RANCH
Under the
RIMROCK

" . . . *Though tourists come in increasing numbers, Central Oregon has managed so far to retain much of its dominant character, which is the loneliness of infinite distance, of endless rimrock, of solitary buttes that are black one moment, purple the next; of tortured canyons, of shimmering waters, of deserts where the wind makes melancholy music on the telephone lines.*

"In this haunted country, you see stray rattlers curled up on great hunks of red lava, watched by magpies, and always overhead are the all-seeing eyes of the circling buzzards. Then, driving down from a plateau of nothingness, you come suddenly . . . to the celebrated McCall Ranch stretching along the Crooked River. The abrupt change is startling. So is the main ranch house, a New England colonial type of manorial size, set at the base of high rimrock.

"In this house, before the highways came, five McCall children were reared. . . . Here they had their own brass band, own newspaper. This self-sufficiency of the McCall Ranch was due in large part to the typical isolation of Central Oregon . . ."—Lincoln-Mercury Times

Stewart Holbrook

—Like the McCalls, a New Englander in birth, but a Westerner in residence.

RANCH
Under the
RIMROCK

By

DOROTHY LAWSON MCCALL

Binfords & Mort, *Publishers*

Portland • Oregon • 97242

Ranch Under the Rimrock

Printed in the United States of America

Third Printing 1971

Dedicated to Hal

Contents

"*In singing the praises of Oregon, I make no qualifications, absolutely none. For I believe there is no place in all the world which holds as many advantages for man, be he young or old, rich or poor, as Oregon.*

"*I came here over eight weeks ago—came to stay three or four days. If it were possible, I would stay on and on and longer. Sixty days' investigation of a country as vast as Oregon may not mean as much to some, but as I have done it, on the go from early morning till late at night, living almost all the time in automobiles, I feel I know your possibilities better than many of you who have lived with them all of your lives.*

"*Would to the Lord I had found it earlier, but I thank Him that I have found it in time to point it to my children. And I pray that He will let me live long enough to see with my eyes that fulfillment of the vision that is as clear to me as yonder snow-capped mountains.*"

Thomas W. Lawson

—Written while visiting the Author—his daughter "Dote"—New Year's, 1914.

Author's Preface

In the early 1900s, Central Oregon was vastly different from what it is today. An area of over 10,000 square miles, its four leading towns at that time were widely separated by great stretches of sagebrush and juniper. This was sheep and cattle country.

Prineville, the seat of Crook County, was the oldest and most flourishing of the towns, with about one thousand inhabitants. Its picturesque courthouse, surrounded by green lawns and tall trees, was an oasis in this dry and dusty region. Prineville's other answer to law and order was the old "Hanging Bridge," which crossed Crooked River two miles west of town. Between 1902 and 1906, many hot disputes of the sheep and cattle wars were settled there by rope instead of law. It has been said that at one time six bodies dangled from its beams.

To the northwest of Prineville, over the towering rimrock, lay Madras. Then a tiny settlement numbering no more than three hundred residents, Madras consisted mostly of homesteaders and dust.

To the southwest was Bend, platted in 1904; it had been a slow grower until 1911 when the railroads were completed. Prior to that, stockmen had driven their animals from summer pasture to market in The Dalles on the Columbia, following the Deschutes River as far as possible. The only place for miles where the Deschutes could be forded was at one graceful curve, from which Bend took its name. Old-timers always spoke of the settlement as "Farewell Bend."

West of Prineville, the town of Redmond—like Madras with a population of about three hundred — was just beginning to emerge. A stark little town with a main street of clapboard buildings, Redmond was important mainly as a trading center until two railroad tycoons fought a costly and spectacular battle while constructing two railroads up the deep, rocky gorge from the Columbia River to Bend.

The region of Central Oregon had remained the same for decades: sagebrush, juniper, dust, cattle drives, small isolated settlements. Then, in 1909, Empire Builders James J. Hill and

E. H. Harriman began their two-year struggle for the right-of-way up a rugged canyon where a saddle horse found it difficult to gain footing. . . . The two giants had been fighting elsewhere for years.

Passenger and freight, combined, scarcely justified two railroads fighting tooth and nail the length of the Deschutes Canyon, only to come to a dead standstill in the grain fields of Central Oregon. But this they did, with construction crews often shooting at each other from opposite sides of the river. When the lines were finally completed, engineers racing down the canyon would wave and thumb their noses as first one train pulled ahead, then the other.

Prineville, however, was still without the railroad for which it had been waiting since its founding by Barney Prine, a blacksmith and saloonkeeper who established squatters' rights on the banks of the Crooked River in 1868. Two years later, a young rancher by the name of Monroe Hodges was to trade a pony and ante up twenty dollars for these rights.

In 1916, frustrated Prineville citizens bonded themselves to build and operate their own railroad. Completed in 1918, it is said to be the only municipally owned railroad in the United States. It extends nineteen miles down Crooked River to connect with a branch of the Union Pacific at Prineville Junction. This railroad runs directly through the McCall ranch today.

For more than fifty years, people from many parts of the world have visited our Central Oregon ranch. And all have been interested in seeing the main house. It was built in 1911 by my father, Thomas W. Lawson of Boston, then a thirty-times millionaire. The house itself is unique: unique because of its sagebrush-and-juniper setting, because of its New-England-furnished interior, and because of its aura of timelessness.

At the end of a three-storied tour through the house, guests step out onto the second-floor balcony. There, spread out in panorama, lie the emerald-green acres of alfalfa. Away to the south looms the opposite rimrock. To the east, beyond Prineville, rise the dusky, misty blue peaks of the Ochocos; to the west, the snow-covered peaks of the mighty Cascades.

Then, from guests, comes the inevitable question: "Would you tell us, Mrs. McCall, how you happened to come to this part of the world?" Now, at seventy-nine years, I cannot continue to answer this question indefinitely, so I have written this story. D. L. M.

Foreword

Several years ago, United States Senator, Mark O. Hatfield, then governor of Oregon, wrote the following:

As Governor of Oregon, I am particularly pleased that Dorothy Lawson McCall has decided to tell the story of how one American family migrated to our state shortly after the turn of the century. Although this family had some advantages of wealth and background, the McCall story is not dissimilar to that of many another eastern family which had pioneered Oregon earlier. Certainly, many of the common hardships that inevitably came to those who settled this country in its early days were shared by this former Boston debutante.

Those who prefer their "Wild West" unadorned by the niceties of civilization may be disappointed to learn that it was possible to have most of the modern conveniences of the day, and to enjoy life largely in the localities. Even the McCall neighbors were surprised at the time. But enjoy life they did, and they continue to do so, for this is a "modern" pioneer story, and the McCalls remain active in business, political, and social life.

Oregon is rich in history, and the McCall family has added to that richness. Our state has seen many "firsts," and thus it is entirely plausible that a five-fireplace, five-bathroom house in Central Oregon should be built by the son of a future governor of Massachusetts, to become the first such edifice in this part of the state.

Because this is, in a sense, a historical work, it may be well to briefly discuss our state's past.

The Spanish mariner, Bruno Heceta, is credited with being the first white person to see the coast of what is now Oregon in 1775. Captain Robert Gray, in his ship the *Columbia,* in 1792 was the first to sail up the river now bearing his ship's name, and storied in song and fable as the "Great River of the West."

Explorations by Lewis and Clark, who wintered on the Oregon coast in 1805-06, led later to the greatest migration of people in the history of the American continent. In the 1840s and 50s, "Oregon or Bust" and the Oregon Trail were on the lips and in the hearts of thousands of hardy pioneers who made the long and difficult overland trip. Some of this same spirit must have motivated Henry McCall when he left a comfortable home and a highly attractive future to move westward with his bride of a few weeks. And, some of the same pioneer perseverance must have been part of his makeup, else the McCall family might have lasted only a short time in this then harsh land.

Out of the early Oregon Country, embracing all of what is now the States of Washington and Oregon, and parts of British Columbia, Idaho and Montana, peopled by Indians and a few trappers, sprang an American territory, and, finally a state, on February 14, 1859. It was here that the first American government on the Pacific Coast was founded, as well as the first American University west of the Mississippi. Oregon has pioneered in the formulation of democratic government processes, establishing the first direct primary, and providing for the initiative, recall, and referendum. It was among the first to enact meaningful civil and social legislation, guaranteeing to all its citizens the rights included in the United States Constitution.

In the 20th Century, Oregon has developed into a great agricultural and industrial state, and leads the nation in lumber production. It is still the land of opportunity to those who would recognize the potential.

Today, we Oregonians compare our state's past to our present way of life and find the relationship meaningful. We are proud of our special heritage. Such stories as that of the McCall family help bridge the gap between pioneer days and the present era, and are well worth telling. More importantly, they are well worth reading.

Dorothy Lawson McCall's long-remembered anecdotes, her warm personal recollections, and her entertaining accounts of not only family happenings but those of Prineville, Central Oregon, and Portland in the early days of this century will, I feel certain, be a source of enjoyment to all who read this book.

May Dorothy Lawson McCall, bride of the man in the "Khaki Pants and a Tall Silk Hat," and matriarch of the proud family, continue to share in the history of our great state.

Mark O. Hatfield

RANCH
Under the
RIMROCK

To M. Granum
Lawrence,

from
Mama & Daddy
and
Best Wishes
from the author

Dorothy Lawson McCall.

The Ranch
December 1,
1972

"*Growing up on the 'Ranch Under the Rimrock' was a memorable and happy experience for all of us McCall children. What might seem like hardships to some—one-room school houses, flooded rivers, work in the hay fields—were exciting challenges and often the occasion for great fun. I only wish more children today could have a comparable opportunity to grow up on such a ranch in a place as wonderful as Central Oregon.*

"*I'm sure Dad—a beloved, gentle man—would be proud of his 'Dote' for having written this book. I know I am.*"

Tom McCall
Governor of Oregon

I. East Is East

"God!" said the old-timer as he spat on the floor, "hardwood floors on 21!"

On Section 21 in the heart of Oregon's sagebrush, a millionaire's mansion was nearing completion three stories high—rooms of palatial size—five fireplaces—five bathrooms. . . . *Five bathrooms in a strictly "privy" area!*

The slogan, "Go West, young man," was resounding across the nation. Fruit ranches in the Great Northwest were being advertised as the real Eldorado. College men from the East were flocking to "God's Country" for summer vacations. They worked on these fruit ranches and in the lumber mills—but the real Eldorado for the effete Easterners was the cattle country.

At that time, to young Hal McCall, fresh out of Harvard, the urge to go west was especially strong.

It was a long jump from Beacon Street, Boston, to the homestead country of Central Oregon. In 1911, Section 21 was 640 acres of rattlesnake-infested sagebrush and juniper. Wild horses roamed that piece of land; coyotes prowled and howled at night. Even so, it was good, irrigable land, and the Crooked River flowed through it. The water rights plus the fine irrigation prospects sold "Section 21" to my millionaire father. He, in turn, presented it to his daughter and son-in-law as a wedding present.

Hal's family and mine had been close friends in Winchester, Massachusetts, for many years, but Hal and I had known each other well only as small children. Wintertime saw very little of the McCalls in Winchester, as the family then lived in Washington, D. C. Hal's father, Samuel McCall, was serving there in the United States Congress, and Hal was away at boarding school. Since our family always spent summers on Cape Cod, the result was that while growing up, Hal and I saw nothing of each other until one lovely spring day when I was fifteen. After starting school in Winchester, Hal was sent to St. Mark's School in Southborough, Massachusetts, where he spent the next eight years.

On that spring day, I had driven up to Southborough to watch a St. Mark's-Groton baseball game. With Hal captain of the team we were all rooting for St. Mark's and were greatly excited over this final game of the season. However, our enthusiasm was short-lived, for St. Mark's lost the game. Afterward, we rooters swarmed over to console the captain of the losing team. As we caught up with him leaving the field, I realized this disheveled character was the blue-eyed little boy who used to drop me off at kindergarten in his pony cart. Simultaneously recognizing me, he smiled. The gloom began to disappear. Then turning to the rest of us, Hal suggested,

"Give me a chance to clean up, and we'll all have dinner together."

During his last year at St. Mark's and the following years at Harvard, Hal and I saw a great deal of each other. Gradually I became impressed with his intense interest in life in the West, for the McCalls' life in Winchester and Washington, D. C., had never included the great, open spaces.

My family knew very little about the West, but once a year the McCalls would be regaled by western stories told by a longtime family friend, Mr. Esterbrook, who would paint glowing descriptions of his mining projects in Idaho. But his stories were not limited to mining alone. He would also bring to life cowboys on galloping horses racing across the range, and fields of golden grain spreading out to the horizon.

2

These western stories of prosperity in the wide, open spaces had made a lasting impression on Hal McCall. Early in life, he made up his mind to see this country for himself someday. In fact, Mr. Esterbrook's stories intrigued all the McCalls, but mining projects in the West and galloping cowboys meant nothing either to me or to my family.

In spite of this, Hal would often say, "Now, when you and I are married, Dote, we'll get out of good old New England and take a chance on the West together. I've got to go out and see that country for myself, and I guess I'll want you to come with me."

Though our following romance—which started at a disastrous baseball game—eventually led to marriage, Hal's first trip was made without me. It was after his third year at college that he finally had a chance to see the West; a friend from Harvard, Harry Corbett, asked him to come out to Portland, Oregon.

In July 1909, with Hal leaving for Portland and my family planning a trip to Europe, it was decided to announce our engagement. Before leaving on our respective trips, Hal and I mapped out our future career. His many years in Washington had amply fitted him for a position in the diplomatic service. This type of life appealed to us both. But to me it seemed that the Portland trip might weaken his interest in life in Washington. This proved to be true.

From his many letters, it was apparent that the West was gradually taking hold of him and he was becoming less and less interested in the plans we had made. One of his letters described at length Colfax, Washington, where he had taken a job through acquaintances in Portland. From then on, Hal's "love letters" were mostly glowing accounts of the "Golden Palouse" country!

Apprehensive, I would write, "I hope this job you have is only for a very few months. I have a dreadful feeling though that once we are in this 'Golden West' you won't want to come back home at all."

3

And Hal would answer, "Let's not cross that bridge until we come to it. It's still quite a way off."

So it seemed at the time. But when Hal came home from the West, it was a very short time before both families were making plans for our wedding.

They finally agreed on the date. And as the time drew near, my doubts and forebodings were completely overshadowed by the excitement of the forthcoming marriage.

The wedding was fully illustrated from the East Coast to the West. This "snow wedding" at Dreamwold* on December 15, 1910, was written up at great length. The following is an excerpt from one of those newspapers:

> A driving snowstorm beat upon the glass-covered veranda as the shadows fell this afternoon at the "snow wedding" of Miss Dorothy Lawson, daughter of Thomas W. Lawson, and Henry McCall, son of Congressman Samuel W. McCall of Winchester.
>
> Miss Dorothy was the third of Mr. Lawson's daughters to marry from Dreamwold, and as her sisters had, one a "harvest wedding," the second a "June wedding," she chose for herself a "snow wedding."
>
> Following the old English custom, the day was a holiday on the Dreamwold estate and the employees joined with the invited guests from the city in the wedding dance. After the honeymoon, the bride and groom will go to Portland, where Mr. McCall will be engaged in business.

---

*Dreamwold was my father's 1,000-acre estate on Cape Cod, Massachusetts.

2. And West Is West

After a brief honeymoon in Maine, Hal and I went back to Dreamwold. Decorations had been left up from the wedding, and the holiday season was in full swing. Festivities spilled over into the New Year.

Since I had never been farther west than New York City, the prospect of crossing the continent fairly overwhelmed me. In spite of this, we started preparing for the trip west. At the last minute we decided to take Nora Daly with us. Nora had been part of our family for many years, filling the role of guardian, housekeeper, and friend. A staunch New England spinster with a great sense of humor and the traditional heart of gold, she had never failed any of us.

Once on our way, this would make for a situation that was unique from the bridegroom's standpoint—a honeymoon with a chaperone! Coming into the dining car late the first morning out, I was greeted by the pleasant head waiter. With a smile, he announced, "Your mother and brother have already breakfasted, Miss."

There was a gay group on hand at the South Station in Boston to wish us well. My last glimpse of those familiar, merry faces was dimmed by tears, and had it not been for Nora's reassuring hand on my arm, I believe I would never have made that trip at all.

Once settled aboard the train and realizing the long-discussed adventure was really beginning, my spirits began to pick up. Scenes from the Pullman windows and from the observation car were exciting—though at times scarcely visible through clouds of thick, black soot.

As we rolled on over the great plains into the Pacific Northwest, and finally into Oregon, the scenery became more and more impressive. But skies grew leaden, and I thought that the gray river and the wet cottonwoods were the most depressing sight I had ever seen. *Where, oh where, was Hal's Golden West?*

When we came into Portland's Union Station, it was a gloomy, drizzly January morning. From the station we drove straight to the Portland Hotel—an impressive edifice on the outside but a bit dreary on the inside. Our room was especially somber, with its heavy hangings and dark lithographs on the wall; one of these pictures I still vividly remember: "Daniel in the Lion's Den." The worst feature of all, though, was a strange contraption called a folding bed, which in those days was even considered dangerous. The built-in treachery of this new type of bed had been played up quite frequently in the news: victims had been folded up without warning; corpses had been discovered in the morning by a shocked chambermaid.

This was the last straw! I delivered a high-pitched ultimatum: we would either have a civilized bedroom, or I would take the next train back to Boston. On this unpleasant note, the honeymooners moved to a more "civilized bedroom"—in the same hotel.

The next morning Hal bought an *Oregonian*, Portland's famous newspaper, then in its sixty-first year of publication. Together we studied the classified ads, only one of which seemed hopeful—"Bungalow on Portland Heights." Hal called the given number, and an agent agreed to meet us there that afternoon. Hal hired a car and, along with Nora, we all set out for the "Bungalow."

Many times since his first trip west, Hal had described Portland Heights to me. He had once said, "I hope sometime, Dote, we will see Portland Heights together, especially in the evening after dark. You will be dazzled!"

And I had answered, "Remember Hal, I once spent six months in Paris. *You* should see Montmartre, especially in the evening after dark!"

Even on a partly cloudy afternoon, Portland Heights is impressive. As we neared our destination, the skies—which had cleared briefly—revealed a breath-taking scene. Below us lay the city of Portland, circled in the distance by snow-capped mountains; to the north was Mt. St. Helens, to the east the glistening peak of Mt. Hood, and in between was the lofty outline of Mt. Adams.

As the clouds closed in again, we came in sight of the "Bungalow." From the distance the little house struck us as a bit dismal. Hal drove the car up to the doorway, and standing there waiting for us was the real estate agent. We all scrambled out of the car and followed him into the house.

What a contrast to the scenic beauty just outside! The interior reeked of wet and mildew. New England Nora seemed overcome by the stale and musty air. Drawing me aside, she said in a loud whisper, "I think something's dead in the basement, Dote, and I'll bet there's been a murder here!" To her dying day, when mentioning her stay in Portland, Nora Daly would shudder and say, "Glory be, Dote, that bungalow!"

Next morning we continued our house-hunting. At the tag-end of the day, thoroughly depressed by all the unattractive two-room apartments, we suddenly stumbled onto the Wickersham, a newly built uptown apartment house. We could scarcely believe it—a spacious apartment with six rooms. The search ended; we had found what we sought.

Although the apartment was more than ample for our needs, it was difficult, especially for Nora and me, to adjust to the confinement of apartment life. Always before, I had spent my time in large houses or the great outdoors. Now, instead of my usual, active winter sports life, my only outside exercise was returning Portland social calls. In the two seasons Hal had spent in the West, he had formed a great many friendships. Now these friends wanted to make his young wife feel welcome also. As was the custom, when calling cards were left, one was expected to return the visit.

In spite of such friendliness, I gradually became restless and unhappy; the rains never seemed to stop. New England's blustery storms were completely different; they were followed by clear skies. In Portland, the rain came quietly down and down—the wind never blew, the sun never shone. As time dragged on, the clouds seemed blacker and the rain wetter.

Apartment living was new for Nora also. She had spent all her life in large New England houses surrounded by gardens. She became despondent and Hal and I both realized we must make a vital decision—Nora must leave us soon, or nostalgic longings would completely overcome her. Having arrived at this conclusion, with Nora's agreement, we bade her farewell at the Union Station and returned to the empty apartment.

Some mornings after Hal left for his bank job, I became so desperate that I'd grab a raincoat and umbrella—still damp from a previous day's outing—and paddle my way down back streets to the Union Station eight blocks away. There I would stand, listening and watching for the Chicago train to pull out for the East. As the train disappeared with a final blast, I'd slosh my way back to our apartment and pick up my daily life.

Although I was depressed by the never-ending rain, life wasn't completely gloomy when Hal was with me. We were constantly being entertained and rarely had a quiet evening together in the apartment. But how we missed the symphony and the theater! And my husband missed his favorite sport. During the first two months we were in Portland, Hal, an expert golfer, managed to play only once—on a rare sunny day in February.

It was not until March, though, that real trouble cropped up. Hal developed an acute pain in his head, and doctors discovered a recurrence of an old frontal sinus injury. They recommended an immediate operation, even though this was quite dangerous at the time. That operation changed the course of our lives, for the doctor's ultimatum, "no office life for three months and plenty of rest and sunshine," sent us looking for sunshine . . . sunshine from Portland skies?

While Hal was convalescing, friends told us about Mrs. Alma Howe's Cottage Farm Resort in Hood River, the only place of its kind in 1911 within commuting distance of Portland. Motels had not come into being then, and resorts were few and far between. The Cottage Farm was situated in the midst of an orchard with individual cottages scattered among the trees. These cottages were for families with children. The main house, a large, simple farm-house type, furnished lodgings for adults only.

The day we arrived, Mrs. Howe showed us to our room—one of white-washed walls and plain furniture. Sunlight and the smell of apple blossoms streamed in through the open windows, and the distant mooing of a cow was soothing to two tired city travelers.

We were both delighted with the beauty of the Hood River Valley in the spring: fruit trees were budding and the sun was shining in a blue, blue sky. All around, dark evergreen forests stretched out to snow-covered mountains, dominated by Mt. Hood. I thought, *if only we could stay here for the summer instead of going back to that rainy city!* But it was necessary for Hal to keep appointments with his doctors. So, after just three days, we reluctantly left the peace of that valley to return to Portland, where Hal would have to face the confinement of apartment life without a job.

The doctor's ultimatum had been, "No more office work for

at least three months." Despite my premonitions, however, the Portland apartment appeared comfortable and cozy. The winter rain was beginning to slacken and there were signs of spring: crocuses were peeping out, and camellias and rhododendrons would soon bloom. It would not be long before Portland would become the "City of Roses."

About this time, Mrs. Alexander Morrison came to the apartment. I was standing on a stool, hanging curtains, when there was an unexpected knock on the hall door. No buzzer had warned me of a visitor. I stepped down and hurried to open the door. There she stood—a breath of New England—in a black-tailored suit and black-tailored hat.

"You must have been surprised," she quickly explained, "but I followed someone else in. I'll only stay a moment. My husband, Dr. Morrison, is rector of Trinity Church, just around the corner. You'll recognize the rectory by its spreading green lawn. Hal has told me you are not used to apartment living, so whenever you are in the mood, just slip over whether we are home or not." That "slip over" began a life-long friendship between the Morrisons and the McCalls.

Life was looking up! On sunny days, Hal and I drove into the Tualatin Valley with a rented horse and carriage. The valley reminded us of home, especially our old courting grounds, the Burlington Hills which stretch out from Winchester to Concord and Lexington.

Coming back from a trip to the valley one day, we found a letter from father. It brought good news: he was coming to Portland with my younger sister Bunny. Hal was excited, but I was ecstatic. After father's letter, Hal and I began making plans. The timing of the visit was fortunate as Rose Festival week was coming up, and the Morrisons were invaluable in helping us. Another good friend, Mrs. Helen Ladd Corbett—who had visited us at Dreamwold—was also very helpful.

"What in heaven's name, Dorothy, are you going to do with

all these people? You can get a room out for the maid, and your sister can stay here with you and Hal. But knowing your father, I can't picture him condensed in this apartment. Send him over to 293 6th Street (the Corbett home), and we'll put him up in his usual spacious fashion."

"But Mrs. Corbett," I said, "Hal and I have already worked out the housing problem, and what none of you know is that we have a big surprise for all of you. When our baby is born, I will be the first of father's four daughters to have a child, and I am sure he will want to be near us."

Anticipating the arrival of our first child, Hal and I had hired a cook. Her name was Delia Dorman. We thought she was joking when she told us her husband was a burglar—"But," she added, "we have not lived together for some time." This fact did not dampen our enthusiasm; however, it did add color to our apartment living. Delia, with all her oddities, proved a jewel.

Sometimes, after dark, there would be rumors of a prowler around our neighborhood. Delia, a little round woman with gleaming eyes and pugged-up hair, would always become greatly excited. She would invariably call to Hal, "Mr. McCall, Mr. Mc-Call, where's your rifle, where's your .22?"

"What do you want it for, Delia?" Hal would call back.

"Just in case," she would say cryptically.

After many false alarms, one very hot evening, before the family arrived, we had a real alarm. A third-floor tenant reported seeing the phantom prowler in the flesh; he was skulking on the fire escape. All hands converged on the sidewalk in front of the Wickersham; police cars were on the way. At the height of the excitement, Delia appeared. Forging her way through the crowd with Hal's .22 under her arm she cried, "Let me at him! I bet that's Dorman." The prowler was finally flushed out, but he was not her errant husband.

11

Shortly after this, my family arrived, to be welcomed with open arms. When the excitement finally subsided, though, father calmly announced he could stay only three weeks.

"But, Pa, we thought you were going to stay all summer," I wailed; and Hal added, "We've so much to show you, Mr. Lawson." Show them we did, with the result that father and Bunny never left the west for three months.

It was June and the Rose Festival was just starting. Roses were everywhere. Friends brought bouquets of flowers to the apartment; and there were invitations to dinners and interviews. Father's reputation as the Copper King had preceded him, and we were besieged night and day with telephone calls. With so many people trying to sell property, the entire Northwest seemed up for sale.

Gone was the gloom and depression of the early months. Portland was in a Mardi Gras mood, with a Rose Queen and Court and the whirling color of parades and flourish of bands almost around the clock. Climaxing the final day of celebration was a Rose Festival parade of flower-decked floats bearing lovely girls in fanciful costumes.

The week following the Festival we made arrangements for a short trip to Hood River so that Father, Bunny, and the youngest Morrison daughter, Jean, could see the valley with fruit trees in blossom. Jean and Bunny had become firm friends at first sight. As we drove up from the station, my father was visibly impressed by the countryside. Mrs. Howe, of the Cottage Farm Resort, met us at the door of the main house.

Every day we drove around the valley looking over ranches. Father was so impressed that he toyed with the idea of investing in Hood River property, but Hal was skeptical; cattle-raising was his idea, and he was anxious to be off to Central Oregon and the cattle country.

On our trips through the valley it was horrifying to see Father walk up to the door of a prosperous-looking home and ask, "How much would you take for this place?" But in those declining boom days, we found no one unwilling to sell on the spot.

Mrs. Howe fascinated Father with her knowledge of Indians and Indian lore. She spoke the language of the Indians and understood their temperament. One evening, she called to Father to come and meet old "Indian George." She had known George for years; he was her special charge and always welcome. No one knew his age but it was rumored that he was well over one hundred years old. Almost totally blind, he was still able to get about the valley and was widely respected for his store of knowledge.

When Mrs. Howe introduced the two men, she watched their reactions. Indian George seemed unimpressed with the millionaire "Copper King" from Boston, but my father seemed greatly impressed with the old Indian. As they talked, Mrs. Howe interpreted the guttural Indian speech. Two words caught Father's ear: "Boston Man." Flattered and pleased, my father turned to Mrs. Howe and exclaimed, "Amazing! Think of being recognized by this old Indian so far from Boston!" Ruefully, Mrs. Howe replied, "Mr. Lawson, I'm sorry to disillusion you, but in the Indian language 'Boston Man' means white man." Never before had I seen my famous father so deflated!

Warm christmas wishes to
Lawrence

Gov. Tom McCall

3. Prineville Routs the "Silver Lake Indians"

Soon after the meeting with Indian George, we returned to Portland to prepare for a promised visit with the Sharps in Central Oregon. Before we left the apartment, Hal warned us the trip would be hot and rugged. "Wear as few clothes as possible. I'm just wearing a shirt and pants."

We Bostonians were horrified. No traveler ever left the North or South stations in such informal clothes, but how we wished we had taken his advice as the day wore on . . . especially after leaving the Columbia River and its lush growth, to turn south along the Deschutes River.

In hot weather, a train trip up the Deschutes Canyon was indescribably uncomfortable. As the canyon narrowed, the heat grew worse and worse. Babies cried and whimpered. Bunny and I pulled off all the clothes we decently could—gloves, collars, jackets, shoes. We still panted. Hal wasn't around to say, "I told you so," because before leaving the Union Station, Carl Grey, President of the Union Pacific, had discovered that Father was aboard and had sent a conductor to invite him to his private car. Females were left in the day coach surrounded by youngsters and orange peels.

In late afternoon, the canyon opened out, the track leveled off, the air cooled, and we rolled out into the grain fields of Central Oregon. In the distance we could see the snow-capped mountains—the Three Sisters and the great white peak of Mt.

Jefferson outlined in the gorgeous sunset. At three thousand feet the air was delightfully cool.

Tom Sharp, who managed the Corbett high country ranches, met us at Redmond with his car. As dusk fell, we jounced over bumpy roads toward the ranch country where Hal and I were to live and raise our five children. Limitless distances dwarfed the small clapboard houses along the way. Seen dimly in the gloaming was breathtaking scenery, but underfoot, dust boiled up around the car. Hal's vision of the West was there, though: broad fields with their acres of crops.

As we drove through the cool of the evening to the Sharps, I was still unprepared for the realities of ranch life. I expected a huge house set in acres of green fields, with lovely foliage around it. The small house we finally reached was disappointing, at least its exterior was.

Margaret Sharp—a handsome young woman with a ready smile, deep blue eyes, and the happy faculty of making everyone feel at home—met us at the door. We stepped into a pleasant living room lined with books and warmed by an open fire. Tom had "batched" in the remodeled house when it was cabin-sized, before his marriage. Margaret showed Father to the small, simple guest room he was to occupy, the only other part of the original building; then invited him to join us on a tour of the other rooms.

The dining room door was thrown open. What a contrast to the guest room! Vast and high ceilinged, it was paneled in a dark wood more suitable to an English manor than a ranch house. Bearskin rugs were scattered on its polished floor. The room looked as if it should be in a royal shooting lodge, with trophy heads mounted around its walls.

"You won't believe this," said Tom, who was known for his elaborate exaggerations, "but before I could marry Margaret and bring her up here, the ranch foreman and I had to build this addition. The paneling is from appleboxes, stained."

16

"You must have eaten a lot of apples," said Hal, giving me a wink. Amid the ensuing laughter, Margaret opened the door into the next room. What a sight met our eyes! The "master bedroom" was a duplicate of the overly impressive dining room. It was furnished with a double bed and two cots, which took care of the ladies—but what about the remaining men? Hal was invited to share a pup tent in the yard with Margaret's brother Alec, and Tom planned to drape himself on a couch in the living room.

For the Sharps to welcome so many guests in such a situation was great hospitality, but I was to learn this was a hospitable country.

After a late snack in front of the open fire, the Sharps gave us a description of the coming week-end festivities in Prineville. The town would be literally bursting at the seams. From all over the surrounding ranch country, people would be crowding in for two reasons: the Central Oregon Development League was meeting over a three-day period, and excitement over the annual series of ball games was running high. Betting would hit the ceiling with large sums of money changing hands before the end of the celebration. My father pricked up his ears.

Next day, as we drove through the Crooked River Valley toward Prineville, I only half listened to the conversation, so intent was I on absorbing the passing landscape. It was a brilliant morning and I looked at the valley with a new light. The night before we had been tired from our long, hot trip. Today was a fresh experience.

Oregon ranch country in early summer is unbelievably beautiful—no skies so blue, no sun so bright. First-cutting alfalfa is just beginning to blossom, fence high and emerald green, with millions of butterflies fluttering over purple buds. Great, thriving ranches sprawl on both sides of the road all the way into town. As we passed one field, I saw sleek white pigs, big and little, and marvelled at them—clean, wandering loose in large patches of green. As a small child in Winchester, Massachusetts, a pig to me meant a shadowy mastodonic creature kept under a barn, grunting and wallowing in eternal twilight.

The outlying desert was just as lovely, for the sage has a deerskin finish and the junipers a fresh new-grown look. The eye follows almost limitless alfalfa fields, towering rimrock, and great stretches of sage and juniper to faraway horizons.

When we reached Prineville, a throng of holiday seekers crowded the main street; bands blared, balloons floated from children's outstretched arms, and flags fluttered from wires strung across the dusty street. Because it was nearing game time, we drove directly to the field, a sand-lot diamond on the outskirts of town. We were all in a betting mood as we settled ourselves on the grassy edge of the field.

Indignation was added to excitement when word got around that the visiting Silver Lake Indian team was actually Gus Schroeder's Sheepherders, comprised of eight members from an outstanding Portland baseball club and one Silver Lake Indian. The ninth man had missed the train, so the resourceful Schroeder picked up the young Indian who had drifted into Prineville for the celebration. Gus convinced him that he would make a star center fielder out of him.

When it came time to write the Indian's name in the batting order, no one could translate the guttural sounds which emanated from his mouth; but inasmuch as they sounded something like "Luke Magluke," that name was given him during the series. "Luke Magluke" made a great center fielder, and at the end of the first day, the Sheepherders emerged the winners.

At an indignant meeting after the game, Hal McCall, the great Harvard second baseman, was "discovered" by the Prinevillites and signed up for the last two games.

We Prineville rooters roared into town early the second day, anxious to back up our team and our boy. I like to think our enthusiastic support helped win that second game, for win it we did, tying the series 1-1.

On the morning of the third and last day, we were in a fighting mood—as were most of the Central Oregonians. Prineville smarted under the "Silver Lake Indian" deception. In the town, competition had become vicious. People on the high side of the mountains, as well as our little group from the low, felt that the ranch country had been "taken for a ride."

The betting was fast and furious as game time approached. Prineville had a slight edge on the visitors and we were convinced that Hal was responsible. A leading citizen, Doc Rosenberg, was busy taking bets which ranged from money to horses, cattle, mules, and baled hay. Naturally Father was betting heavily on Prineville; partly out of loyalty to the town, but also because of his admiration for his son-in-law's baseball skill. The game started before the largest crowd in the history of Prineville baseball, where it was not unusual for fans to travel over a hundred miles or more to see "their" team play against visiting teams.

To the surprise of everyone, the Sheepherders unleashed a batting bombardment in the first inning. They kept it up to the extent that at the end of the fourth inning they led 9-0. Prineville fans began to feel like the fans in "Mudville" when the Mighty Casey struck out, and it seemed apparent that there would be "no joy in Prineville" that night.

But Father, the optimist, was sure Prineville would come through. He casually handed Tom a crumpled greenback asking him to take it to the stake-holder. Before reaching Doc Rosenberg, Tom uncrumpled the money and discovered it was a thousand-dollar bill. He rushed back to Father and asked, "Haven't you made a mistake, Mr. Lawson, on the amount you want to bet? You're really crazy to throw this much into the pot with Prineville so far behind."

Father assured him that he knew how much he was adding

to what he had previously bet on Prineville, and that the odds would be even more in his favor. When our team came to bat in the fifth inning, strange things happened to the Sheepherders. All of them, especially the pitcher and infielders, seemed to have lost their energy. The southpaw pitcher afterwards explained that he suddenly had no pep or control, and all he had on the ball was a "prayer."

Prineville batters had a field day. Errors were rampant as the Sheepherder infield booted the ball around. When the fifth inning ended, Prineville had five runs. The malady which had so suddenly seized the Sheepherders was explained after the game to have been the high Central Oregon altitude. Also blamed was the alkaline drinking water—otherwise known as whiskey.

The pitcher for the Sheepherders begged his teammates to replace him, but they refused, saying they were in as bad condition as he. The only player on their team who apparently wasn't suffering the vapors was "Luke Magluke." He was used to the "high altitude." During the rest of the game, the fleet-footed Luke, playing centerfield, was kept busy retrieving balls hit over his head. These became lost in the thick sagebrush to such an extent that at one point all of the balls had been used and the game was delayed until more balls could be brought from uptown.

The game ended with Prineville winning 10-9. And of course the happy ending of the game removed Prineville from the "Mudville" category caused by Mighty Casey striking out. For years after the game, when two or more Prinevillites were together, the stirring events of that game would be discussed, and inevitably the "fool bet" by Father would be analyzed and dissected. Echoes of it still reverberate.

The eight so-called "Silver Lake Indian" ballplayers were on the train the next day when we climbed aboard to go back to Portland. One prominent "Indian" told us bitterly about "the altitude" and how he had been practically poisoned by the water.

Knowing full well their part in the great celebration—having watched how it affected their team—we roared with laughter. "When and where did any of you drink water?" Hal wanted to know.

During the Central Oregon visit, Hal and Father looked into ranch prospects. The Sharp ranch (Rancho Escondido) was one of those owned by Harry Corbett. Before we left for Portland, Father suggested that Hal sound out Tom Sharp about the possibilities of buying the Corbett undeveloped Section 21 across the road from them. He had grasped what Hal felt about the area and was not only sympathetic but enthusiastic. "Anything is for sale if the price is right" was applicable in this case and the business of buying Section 21 was completed in Portland at $75 an acre for the river-bottom land.

Hal's dream had come true.

4. Khaki Pants and a Tall Silk Hat

In Portland, a brilliant young graduate of Boston Tech* was engaged to draw up plans for the house and these were sent back for Father's approval. Unfortunately those plans were expanded to fit Father's lavish ideas. Having given my five sisters and brothers houses in Massachusetts—mostly on Dreamwold's acres—he planned our ranch house along the same lines.

However, buying and developing a thousand acres on Cape Cod was quite different from buying and developing 640 acres of sagebrush in the West. For generations, land in Massachusetts had been producing. In building Dreamwold, bit by bit, many small, well-developed properties could simply be brought together into one big estate. When Dreamwold was completed, seven miles of white fence covered with red roses surrounded its thousand acres, and its fertile lands were dotted with many fine buildings and priceless stock.

Developing the western ranch was an entirely different story. Land had to be cleared, leveled, and finally seeded to a rye crop. This was plowed under, and only then was the land ready for irrigation and the seeding of alfalfa and grain. Pipe was laid from the irrigation pump installed in the river. By early fall, operations were finally under way on the ranch.

*Massachusetts Institute of Technology was in Boston at that time, but was later moved to Cambridge.

In the Portland apartment, Hal and I began making plans for the trip home for the Christmas holidays. This would be a memorable occasion for us as we were expecting our first child soon. November 1911 saw us on our way east. On December 6, the baby, Harry, was born at Dreamwold.

In the meantime, work continued at the ranch at high speed under the direction of a capable foreman.

In the spring we left for our Oregon ranch, stopping off at Mrs. Howe's because our house was not quite finished. This time we took a cottage. Not only did we have the baby and a hardy English maid named Mabel; we also had Miss Minnie I. Haggart, the baby's nurse since birth. Miss Haggart* came to stay three months and lived with us the rest of her life. Weathering all our ups and downs through the years—to our five children and all who knew her she became the beloved "Miss Ha."

Father had insisted on sending Miss Haggart with us saying, "I don't want you going out to that rattlesnake country with a baby you don't know how to take care of. After all, you know nothing about babies or rattlesnakes. Miss Haggart is an obstetric nurse—the best. She might not know anything about rattlesnakes, but she's already taken care of sixty-three babies and has the sense that God gave her."

On the other hand, we sometimes worried about Mabel. In Boston, one of her main duties had been to brush my hair for an hour every night. Her life on the ranch, however, was to prove far different from what she had previously experienced. Nevertheless she had insisted that she wanted to be with her particular pet, "Miss Dorothy"—though Hal and I privately suspected she was interested in single men in the West. It was comfortable having her around, even though she was a tremendous liar. Whenever she was caught up, she threw her arms overhead and exclaimed, "As sure as there's a God in Heaven!" . . . to which I'd answer, "Now I *know* you're lying."

---

*Miss Haggart was a stalwart Canadian woman, a graduate of Massachusetts General Hospital in Boston.

Before leaving Portland the preceding November, we had put our apartment furnishings and wedding presents in storage. Now these were all shipped to Redmond by rail, and Father had added many other treasures from Dreamwold and our Boston town house.

After spending one night in Hood River, Hal left his little family there and went on to Redmond to take the shipment to the ranch. Several days later I received a long-distance call from Portland. It was Mrs. Corbett. In those days, long-distance calls in Hood River were something of a rarity. The voice of the operator alarmed me.

Anxiously I asked, "What's happened? Is anything wrong?"

"Anything wrong! Have you seen the papers?"

"We have had no papers here today." I was becoming panic stricken.

"Is Hal there?" Then she stopped, "Oh, of course not."

I fairly shouted, "Mrs. Corbett, is Hal dead?"

Her low laugh was reassuring. "Of course Hal isn't dead, but I think you should know that everything you own has burned in Redmond."

Knowing the deadly force of fire, the news that "everything we owned" had burned in Redmond meant very little to me at the time. The family was still intact.

It was not until several days later—when Miss Haggart and I, with the baby, arrived in Redmond—that we learned all the grim details of the fire. Hal met us at the station, and on the way to the ranch, he retold the story of that disastrous night. . . .

The morning the massive shipment of our household furnishings from the East arrived in Redmond, Hal was on hand to meet it. He explained to the young man in charge of the local freight company that once the goods were taken from the railroad cars and loaded on the horse-drawn wagons, they must be delivered to the ranch immediately. This was imperative. All goods were insured while in the railroad cars; all goods were insured after reaching the ranch; but not one single item could be insured during the rugged desert crossing to the final destination. Unfortunately, Hal could not stay to see these instructions carried out. He was staying at the Sharps' when the morning telephone call reached him.*

Three wagon loads had been sent to the ranch and the goods unloaded on the porch. The drivers returned to Redmond to pick up the remaining three wagons. To these wagons—filled with books, paintings, Irish linens, a grandfather clock, a piano, and a large mahogany chest of Tiffany silver—the young man directing the operation added 280 gallons of gasoline. This additional freight was destined for his company in Prineville. Since our ranch was halfway, this move would save him mileage, but it automatically cancelled all our insurance.

It was dusk before they were ready to set out for the ranch and young Smith, fearing that the valuables might be damaged in the failing light, made a fateful decision. He directed the drivers to cross the road and tie up beside a barn for the night. The barn had been sold recently and the insurance had not been transferred.

It was later that Hal learned more from one of the drivers of the ill-fated wagons. He had awakened to a bright light in the sky and the screaming of terrified horses. Without pulling on even a pair of pants, he raced to the wagons, hoping to release the brakes and roll the wagons free. But the intense heat of the burning gasoline had melted the brakes onto the wheels. In the ensuing holocaust, horses and barns went up in the smoke.

Hal dashed into Redmond the next morning when the news reached us. In place of the former barn, horses, and wagons, there lay a dismal expanse of ashes. At a breath, outlined objects turned into thin air. In the midst of all this devastation only one small object remained intact—a baby's pink porcelain powder-puff jar made in Germany! When Hal realized the ex-

---

*There was only part-time telephone service in Central Oregon at this time.

tent of the damage and the futility of salvaging anything from the flames, he hurried back to the ranch hoping to find something of value in the shipments that had arrived.

These three wagons had been unloaded on the front porch. We tore the boxes open. A large, impressive crate contained a new kitchen wash boiler! The second revealed an empty suitcase, plus a gentleman's leather hatbox which contained Hal McCall's tall silk hat. He had left Boston for the West with a "bridegroom's trousseau." That day Hal stood on the porch of the ranch house in the only clothes he then possessed—a pair of khaki pants and a tall silk hat.

When we reached the ranch, still more trouble was to come. Because of the high water, we were not able to cross our ford of the Crooked River by car, and one of the ranch hands had arranged to meet us with a hay wagon several miles downriver on a neighboring ranch. While sitting cross-legged on the floor of the wagon with Miss Haggart—now white-faced—beside me, and the baby Harry in my lap, I watched Hal and Bob, our driver, swing the horses into the angry river and start across. Midway, one of the team faltered.

"Damn this Taylor mare!" shouted Bob, I knew she'd balk, Mac. She's the only horse that came out when Taylor drove a team through the river awhile back!"

Miss Haggart and I listened horrified. Round and round we swirled, water seeping in through the cracks of the hay wagon. The mare crouched, shivering against her teammate Black Barney; that big horse, straining every muscle to answer to the shouts and curses of Bob, tried to keep the wagon moving.

The movement of the wagon must have spurred the mare. Regaining her courage, she started to pull alongside her mate. The team finally landed us safely on the other side. It was the first I had seen of the house from the time we had marked its site with Hal's handkerchief tied to a bush.

27

Margaret met us at the door, carrying a kerosene lamp, and together we went through the rooms. Margaret's imagination and exuberance were catching as she would exclaim, "And think what we can do with this room, Dote!" We weren't to get electricity for another year.

Before leaving Boston, I had written a description of furnishings for the whole interior, down to the pins in the pin cushion. The next morning Miss Haggart and I checked through the list and found two thirds of the furnishings in every room had been burned.

5. Irrigation, Gophers, and a Swinging Bridge

Digging out after the fire was not our only difficulty that first summer on the ranch. We owned 640 acres of ranch land, but we also owned 640 acres of ranch problems.

Water was the first of these and one that had to be solved immediately. Hal McCall was, I believe, the first rancher to use scientific irrigation in Central Oregon. He had a 400-acre water right on our 640 acres of Crooked River bottom land, and here he established the Dutch "check system" of irrigation.

This water turned dry acres into producing green fields. Water was pumped from Crooked River through a large pipe into the main canal-sized ditch. It was then diverted into sections of field called "checks." A box-like contraption released the water when a sliding board was raised. When water lay level on the check, the board was clamped down and water was forced on to another check, until the whole ranch was well irrigated. This process was put into operation twice, sometimes three times a year.

That first year we operated the pump with a gasoline engine. During our second year, when an independent power company moved into Central Oregon from Spokane, we thought our worries were over. Then came the bills! The power company charged $1,800 during an irrigation season, whether the water was used one month or five. This was an exorbitant charge for two or three months' use of pumps.

Scientific irrigation was not easy. Hal stalked the ditches day and night, shovel in hand; sometimes on foot, sometimes on a horse. Water had to be allocated when and where needed. Occasionally on moonlit nights he would invite some of the family to come out with him.

One particular night, when my family was visiting us, we three—Hal, Bunny, and I—had quite an adventure. The full moon had just come up over the opposite rimrock, casting a silvery light across the whole valley. When Hal, shovel in hand, reached one of the section boards to change the water, he stopped dead in his tracks. Lying in heavy slumber directly across the board was an enormous skunk! How to waken the sleeper without causing alarm . . .

Hal began whistling and Bunny and I started a low humming. When we found that music had no effect, we decided to walk around a bit. On toward midnight, we came back for a final look at that obstinate fat skunk. As we drew near, that onery animal rolled calmly off the all-important section of board and slowly ambled down the field.

Because of the ravages of gophers, repair work had to be done constantly. The battle was an everlasting struggle. Needless to say, the gophers outnumbered us. We battled them with poison in the fields and in the half acre of lawn around the house. Every morning as I stepped out on the second-floor balcony, there would be new dirt hummocks dotting the lawn. Sometimes even the gophers themselves would be sitting at the edges of their holes practically thumbing their noses at us.

And gophers were not the only pests within the protecting fence of the front lawn. Their little cousins, the chipmunks, developed a taste for my nasturtiums. Fast-blooming and brilliantly colored, nasturtiums had seemed to me to be a defense against the bareness of the yard. Flowers had always been important to me. Even as a small child in Winchester, I would look forward to Sunday mornings, toddling along beside my father as he pruned his roses.

Here at the ranch, a bare picket fence had surrounded a dusty yard infested with chipmunks and gophers. Flowers were no part of the cattle country, except for an occasional desert lily out on the range. Wanting quick results, I had planted nasturtiums. We wanted a lawn when the men had time to work on it, but in the meantime the nasturtiums brought a civilized touch to the area. It had been a great satisfaction to feel that one problem was licked—but the satisfaction was short lived. On one bright summer morning when I stepped out on the porch to admire my flowers, there was not a single nasturtium in sight; nothing but neat little piles of green leaves. Cousin chipmunk had a taste for the pungent flavor.

One morning, shortly after, as I glanced out the back window, I was surprised to see a wagon at the back gate. Opening the window, I called, "Do you want to see Mr. McCall?"

"No," the man on the wagon answered, "I want to talk to you, Mis' McCall."

I had never seen this man before. His bright, flashing eyes and stubble of black beard made him look like a stage character. Sensing I was bewildered, he said,

"I'm your neighbor, Dick Butler, from across the river, Mis' McCall. The morning stage left these crates of strawberries for you. I thought they might spoil in the sun."

I was amazed at the stranger's concern. "Oh, Mr. Butler, you needn't have gone to all that trouble!"

With a ready smile, Dick Butler answered, "What's a neighbor for, Mis' McCall?"

Dick Butler proved what a neighbor was for. He was one of the great Tygh Valley horsemen. Without his advice and cooperation down through the years, the McCall children would never have acquired such skill with horses as they had on the western ranch. The bond of friendship formed that day at the back gate with the Butler family continues on through a second generation.

Despairing of ever seeing a lawn around the house, I was more than ever determined to surround our home with trees, shrubs, and flowers; but added to problems with gophers and chipmunks was lack of water. The intense heat, with absolutely no shade, burned every green thing I planted. It was impossible to irrigate our yard as the Sharps had irrigated theirs. They had a small house with no foundation. They irrigated their fields three times a season and always included the lawn. Our big house, standing on a rise, was built over a cement basement. Because of this, field irrigation was impossible. Hal, though, had solved this problem through hydrants. There were four of them in the yard equipped with connections for both regular hoses and fire hoses. The latter, besides fire protection, furnished unscientific irrigation for the yard. Eventually, with this unique method, we were able to flood our yard when necessary. With enough water, flowers could be planted as well as grass, bushes, and trees.

One hot afternoon, coming in from riding and tossing off my coat, I went out into the yard in my riding pants and shirt sleeves to do some digging. At the time Central Oregon was primarily a riding country, but women usually wore only divided skirts. A woman in pants was a great shock. While digging in the yard that hot afternoon this was brought home to me quite forcibly.

"For heaven's sake, will you please get out of that yard and go inside," Hal flung at me as he hurried around the corner of the house.

Completely dumfounded, I followed him. As soon as we were inside, I answered angrily, "What in the world is this all about?"

Hal retorted, "Don't you know that men out here have never seen a woman in pants? Didn't you notice that the field in front of the house is being seeded? The man who's supposed to be doing the seeding is doing absolutely nothing. He has simply been sitting out there gawking at you. Now I will have to seed the whole field over!"

Hal's comment on "woman in pants" had never occurred to me, though I had noticed the divided skirts worn by the women in the West. When I left Boston, women were still riding side-saddle. Cross-saddle riding had come into vogue in England, but even in Massachusetts, women in modern riding pants were still being barred from bridle paths in the East.

We had telephone service the first summer on the ranch and could call Prineville for supplies, but the only means of delivery was a mail stage that ran daily along the opposite side of the river. However, there were no bridges across the Crooked River between the ranch and Prineville. The only way to cross over the water at that time was on a high cable strung from one bank to the other. Hanging from the cable was a narrow board seat. A man would perch on this swinging seat carrying an empty gunny sack and pull himself hand over hand across the river. With the arrival of the stage, the gunny sack would be filled with the groceries, and secured under the hanging seat.

When ladies crossed, they were not asked to use this rugged method, but were seated like high-circus aerialists and swished across the rushing water at high speed. This unique mode of transportation was powered by a man racing through a grain field pulling the other end of the rope.

Later this primitive operation was replaced by a swinging bridge modeled after the kind often used by the Forest Service. It was made of woven wire with sturdy planks for flooring and wire mesh sides. This type of bridge was strong enough to bear the weight of a saddle pony, but cars and wagons had to be parked on the opposite bank. The apparatus was an improvement over the earlier cable crossing, but still did not give easy access to our ranch.

During the latter part of one summer, there was talk of building a new steel bridge near Prineville. When the news reached the ranchers in Lower Crooked River Valley and the homesteaders back in the hills, they immediately banded together and drew up a petition. The petition asked that the bridge be placed far enough down the valley to give both homesteaders and valley people easier access into town. It would also make the little white country school house on the south side of the river available to school children from across the river.

The petition, however, immediately ran into a snag and the fight was on. Prineville citizens wanted a bridge nearer town, and some of the natives in our vicinity were skeptical of the downriver location. There was also much opposition from the die-hards who resisted any progress or "new-fangled" ideas. The bridge was of vital concern to most of us though, for when the river was up in the spring freshet, no fording was possible. The homesteaders had to go many extra miles through the hills to reach Prineville.

At the height of the controversy, Hal and I decided to invite some of the old-timers over for a sociable evening. Three of these ranchers who would have benefited equally well from use of the steel bridge were the most adamant against the plan. Using ice cream, cake, and coffee as bribes, we gave lengthy explanations of the advantages of constructing the bridge, but we made little apparent headway. The food penetrated, but the talk did not. By midnight, fairly exhausted, Hal and I simultaneously came up with the same query: "Since you all will benefit equally from the construction of this bridge, why won't you sign the petition?" The answer was memorable:

"We dunno, but we're 'spicious."

"East is East and West is West and never the twain shall meet"—how true this was proving to be! We were starting to realize what obstacles we were up against as aliens from the East.

The petition failed and the bridge was eventually built close to Prineville. It still stands today—connecting country lane to country lane—a monument to graft and ignorance.

Irrigation, gophers, and bridges were mostly Hal's problems. Meanwhile, I was facing my own real problems of pioneer housekeeping. Upkeep of the large house didn't particularly bother me. That first year, although we used kerosene and lighted the house with candles, I had women to help. It was the elements outside that caused much of the trouble.

In that ranch country, especially in the spring, there is always dust picked up by a howling west wind that seems to blow daily. And the dust from these ploughed fields! . . . That first summer, I watched two women trying to hang out clothes. Repeatedly, blasts of wind leveled the clotheslines and the clothes fell into the dirt for another washing. It was then that I made a ridiculous statement:

"If I ever have green grass under a clothesline, I'll never ask for anything more!"

That first summer on the ranch we were fortunate in being supplied with a good cook—the Sharps had seen to that. (My own experience had been limited. Before I was married, I had gone to Fannie Farmer's Cooking School in Boston. There, a class of eight girls prepared a luncheon. When it was completed, we all sat down and ate it. It all seemed very simple, but later I missed those seven other pairs of hands.)

In the fall, though, our summertime cook received an emergency call from her family and had to leave the following day. I telephoned Mrs. Alexander Morrison and explained my problem. Since I couldn't leave the ranch, she volunteered to interview cooks for me in Portland. Within a few days she called to say a cook was on the way.

Hal met the train that evening and returned to the ranch with the new cook. He hurried up from the back gate with the woman close at his heels. Suddenly I was looking up into the face of a huge, glowering woman with all the initial charm of an English bulldog.

"I'm Mrs. McCall," I said, introducing myself, "won't you sit down." Easing her massive frame into a chair, she announced: "Well, all I can say is, this must be the last place the Lord made."

"Not quite," I answered icily, "Bend is beyond."

Without batting an eye, she went on, "Where's all them flowers and lovely country the lady in Portland told me about?"

"You wouldn't see any flowers coming up the Deschutes Canyon. Anyhow, this is cattle country."

Then she floored me with, "Well, I ain't seen a cow!"

When I told her she would be cooking three meals a day, with dinner served at noon and a light supper in the evening, with fruit and cookies or cake for dessert, she was outraged: "*Cake! Cake bakers get $40 a month!*" The going wage in 1912 for general cooks was $35.

I called to Mabel. After introducing the two women, I suggested that Mabel show the new cook to her room.

"Am I going to sleep alone?" she surprised me by asking. She then pointed at Mabel, "Can't I sleep with her?"

"Don't tell me you're afraid to sleep alone."

"Well," she answered, "I ain't ever been in country like this!"

Later that night, Hal and I discussed how we were going to get rid of her, but the next morning she didn't look so forbidding. We watched her as, dressed in fresh gingham, she helped Mabel hang out clothes. With the sun shining and the meadowlarks singing, she suddenly seemed all set to stay.

When she came back into the kitchen, I suggested that Hal would take her to the evening train.

"You know, Mrs. McCall, this place ain't so bad in the daylight. If I could go on sleeping in Mabel's room, I wouldn't hear them noises in the night. I'd kind of like to stay on awhile."

"What noises?" I inquired hopefully.

"Oh, barks and some sort o' crying like an animal—*what kind o' animals d'you have round here?*"

"Oh, those . . . they're coyotes—little wolves."

She left that evening.

Eventually the cook problem was solved successfully, and over the years we had many fine women cooking for us. The main problem was that single women were scarce in the ranch country and they were in great demand as wives. In fact, a wife was the most valuable piece of livestock on a ranch. We often lost cooks this way. We also lost Mabel to matrimony within a year—cooks, bridges, irrigation, pests. But Hal never lost heart and somehow his faith infected me.

6. Jack-rabbit Drive

My brother Doug and I, as children in Winchester, had raised rabbits—cuddly, little white bunnies with black-tipped ears and pink eyes. But I was totally unprepared for the western jack rabbit of the sagebrush country. In Central Oregon, people talked a lot about rabbits. Jack rabbits were the curse of the homesteader, often destroying an entire vegetable garden in one night. Never having seen one of these predatory animals, I became interested and began asking questions. The answer was always the same: "You just can't live in this country, Mis' McCall, unless the jack rabbits are done away with."

"But I used to raise rabbits in the East," I would protest.

Astonished at my ignorance, my neighbors would reply indignantly, "Well, you sure wouldn't want to raise this kind of rabbit!"

We had not been settled in the ranch country very long when I saw my first jack rabbit. It was toward evening one day when a long-legged animal came loping across the lawn. I thought it was one of the ranch dogs until I saw the long ears which flapped against its head as it ran. Startled, I dashed toward it. The thing bounded to the fence with incredible speed and leaped over.

I called out to Hal as he came up to the back walk, "What, in heaven's name, is that animal that just ran across the lawn? I've never seen anything like it."

"That animal, Dote, is a jack rabbit and I'm afraid you're going to see a lot more of them out here. Their days are numbered though. We are going to get rid of them. A jack rabbit drive is coming up."

Curious, I asked about the drive. "Are we going on horses or on foot? Do people out here hunt rabbits the way we hunt the fox back East? Are they flushed up in numbers, or do you run them down one at a time?"

Hal was highly amused: he explained the battle between the settlers and the jack rabbits. Homesteaders depended on their gardens as a major source of livelihood. With the coming of spring, as green plants poked up above the ground, hordes of jack rabbits would be on hand. Barking dogs were some help, but not a real solution. The hardy jack rabbit was indomitable. He would continue to come back, over and over again. Shotguns had some effect, but poison was out of the question because of domestic animals. The homesteader, then, was forced to solve the problem in his own way—a brutal jack rabbit drive.

"If it's brutal, Hal, I don't suppose women ever go along on the drive?"

"Women certainly do." Hal went on to give me a brief description of the event. Details were carefully planned beforehand. Women who were able to leave home chores and children joined the men at dawn on the morning of the drive. All were armed with sticks and clubs: sticks for flushing the rabbits and clubs for the final slaughter.

As Hal finished, I began to wonder if I would want to join such a primitive excursion. However, a few days later, when I had made up my mind to go along, Hal and I tramped up into the hills just before daybreak to join the jack rabbit "army" in the high brush country. It was still dark when we reached the waiting group. Everyone was in gay spirits; there was much friendly banter along with many rough, country jokes.

At the first hint of daylight, word was given to start. The

group spread out into a long, curved line, forming a solid wall for the attack. It was a cold, crisp morning, and we were all glad of our heavy clothing and stout boots. The line moved slowly forward, everyone beating the sagebrush with clubs and sticks. Frightened and bewildered, rabbits popped up, bounding in all directions. Helter-skelter, individual rabbits would attempt a break-through, first to one side, then to the other, but the marching line was too long for them, and it was gradually closing in for the kill. Slowly but surely and ever narrowing, it converged on the terrified animals, driving them relentlessly into a corral, sturdily fenced and wired beforehand to prevent any escape.

As the sun rose and the light increased, I realized that I would not be able to finish the drive; but I hated to admit, even to myself, that I was unable to keep up with these sturdy people. I commenced to lag behind.

When the first rabbits were forced into the corral, I heard a dreadful sound, a high-pitched squeal of agony. Dimly outlined through the dust, human shapes loomed in the corral. Then I knew what the noise was: the ranchers were clubbing the animals to death. Turning away from that murderous group, I started running for home. It was a long trek; twice on the way my strength gave out, along with my stomach. After several reconstructive intervals, I reached the back gate, where I collapsed.

When Hal came back to the ranch, a bit wobbly himself, he met a white-faced, shaking wife. "It was lucky you went home when you did, Dote, for you never would have lasted through the final annihilation. Every rabbit in that corral was clubbed into a bloody pulp. None of the women stayed for the finish. They started home a little after you left, so don't feel bad about quitting. I would have liked to quit myself. Although the whole thing is appalling to us, we must realize that these drastic measures are necessary. It's just a case of survival between the settlers and the jack rabbits! Two-legged creatures against the four-legged."

Shortly after the rabbit drive, Miss Haggart, Hal, and I were sitting on the screened porch watching the sunset one evening, when we heard a man yelling. Suddenly the bunkhouse door across the way burst open and a man came running over the ditch. He was yelling, "Hi, Mac! Hi, Mac!"

At the time, we had several men working for us; some homesteaders and others living in the bunkhouse. The bunkhouse was a clapboard building—*Gunsmoke* and *Dodge City* style—common in the West in those days. Over the door, the men had nailed a sign, *Kentucky Club,* a popular brand of whiskey.

Hal jumped to his feet as the man approached. Just then we heard loud shouts from the direction of the bunkhouse. The shouting grew louder and I suddenly realized it was Saturday night and a drinking bout was probably under way.

Soon we recognized the man as Lou Ogden, one of the homesteaders on the rabbit drive; also on our payroll. He was waving his arms wildly and was fairly flying when he reached us.

"For heaven's sake, Lou," Hal called, "what's going on over there?"

"The cook's run amuck. He's waving a carving knife and has herded all the men in one corner and swears he's going to cut out their 'liver and lights.' You've just got to get over there right now, Mac."

As Hal started out, I caught hold of his shirt sleeve. "Don't go, Hal. Don't go over there." Paying no attention, he shook me loose and hurried toward Ogden.

As Hal and Ogden disappeared across the ditch, I turned to Miss Haggart, "Oh, why did we ever leave Boston!"

For the next few minutes nothing happened. Suddenly all the men came pouring out. Two of them ran toward the barn. In a short time, with horses hitched to a wagon, they drove up to the front of the bunkhouse. Shoving a mummy-like form into the wagon, they hurriedly drove away.

As Hal came back, I ran out to meet him.

"What happened?"

He grinned. "Well, you people never saw such a sight as that bunkhouse. The men were huddled in a corner, and the cook, drunk as a skunk, was threatening them with a carving knife. I sidled over to the corner and muttered, 'Someone throw me a rope.' Then I threw the rope over the cook's head, started winding and pulled it tight. Well, now he's in the wagon you saw and on his way to the Redmond jail."

Hal paused, then burst into a loud laugh. "If there's one thing I learned at Harvard, it's how to handle drunks!"

7. The First Christmas and Homesteaders

The first Christmas on the ranch was a memorable one; the big house then really came into its own.

The wood in the downstairs fireplaces crackled. The halls, living room, and dining room were lighted with candles. Floors were freshly waxed, rugs rolled away. Here the children could play and dance without disturbing the grownups.

For a month, packages had been pouring in from family and friends in the East. But Father's shipment outshone them all! On that Christmas, Father in Boston took over for Santa Claus. The playthings great and small that rolled into the ranch that year might just as well have come from Santa Claus's North Pole!

One of Boston's leading toy stores made the huge upstairs playroom come alive with large, stuffed animals: a bear, a lion, a buffalo, a giraffe, a camel, and an elephant. The animals all moved on small wheels, making their unique sounds all in different keys. The elephant was large enough to give a ride to good-sized children—and give rides he did!

As soon as word of our Christmas celebration had spread through the valley and to the homestead country, we were assured of a "full house." There was great activity at the ranch on the day before Christmas, as we prepared for the big occasion. Besides getting the house ready, we were busy trimming the tree and preparing great quantities of cakes, cookies, and homemade ice cream. A huge Christmas pine from the Bend country was placed in the living room before the north windows. People driving up and those on the ranch could enjoy the tree all through the holiday season.

Christmas Eve was carried out in true New England style. We were all up most of the night doing last-minute jobs for the big day. On a white, snow-sprinkled sheet at the base of the tree, "Santa and his helpers" busily arranged the presents. Others stuffed gaily colored cornucopias with various sweets—chocolate peppermints, caramels, and hard candies. Large glass and china bowls on the sideboard were filled to their brims with sugared and spiced confections. Some of these delicacies were hung from the tips of the limbs of the tree or tucked in among the full branches.

In Winchester, Massachusetts, there had been many different-length stockings hanging in front of the fireplace; but on that first Christmas at the ranch, there was only one small sock above the hearth. When the last ornament was safely on the tree, "Mr. and Mrs. Santa Claus" filled that small sock.

On the afternoon of Christmas Day, shortly after we had lighted the tree, neighbors began to arrive with their children in wagons, on horses, and on foot. "Open House" had truly begun. Some even made the trip in cars, for automobiles were beginning to be fairly plentiful in Central Oregon by that time.

While Miss Haggart and I served refreshments, the children danced and played to the gay lilt of piano music. From then on until midnight—music, laughter, and singing brought a rousing Christmas to Crooked River Valley. The sound of mingled voices blending in songs such as "Hark, the Herald Angels Sing" floated from the big house until the last candle had melted, and the fires burned low.

The next day, many of our neighbors, especially the home-steaders, came by to thank us for the Christmas party. All were enthusiastic, and for the first time since settling in Central Oregon, we felt the real warmth and friendliness of this western country. Even at Dreamwold, there had never been a more wonderful Christmas. It wasn't long before we became better acquainted with our homestead neighbors.

Every week or so down from the hills would come a light buckboard. Situated as we were, it was a welcome sight. Sometimes the buckboard contained loads of juniper wood, which they sold to us for $3 a cord (today, $35 a cord). Our furnace, weighing three tons, consumed one cord of wood each week during the winter weather, which sometimes touched 40 below. Even the goldfish froze in their bowls. Besides these loads of juniper wood, these amazing homesteaders furnished us with fresh vegetables from their gardens. When the river was up, the homesteaders with their produce solved many of our isolation problems.

Back in Fanny Farmer's Cooking School in Boston, seafood had been a main dish. But planning three meals a day on the ranch, with no seafood available, took some ingenuity for a native of Cape Cod—even with produce from the homesteaders.

Among the many homesteaders living beyond us over the rimrock and onto Lone Pine Flat, some stand out vividly in my memory today. First and foremost were Grandma and Grandpa Foster. With their son and daughter, they had come to this ranch country from New Hampshire. Here they created a bit of New England in the desert wilderness.

Settling on uncultivated land, the Fosters—like the other homesteaders—were required to work the land and improve (or "prove up") that land in order to keep it. They had to fulfill certain rules and regulations. Land must not lie idle! The hardships were almost unbearable. There were all sorts of enemies with which to contend, not the least of which were the elements: winds, dust, and frost, tempered with moderate rainfall. Added to these adversities was a continuous battle to raise food and crops. There were civet cats and porcupines, not to mention the furtive coyote, which posed an endless headache. To the struggling settlers, Grandma and Grandpa Foster became shining symbols of achievement—and those homesteaders needed a symbol.

The first time that Hal and I met them we were astounded. When Grandma Foster appeared in her doorway, we thought she was the prettiest woman we had ever seen. Even out here in these sagebrush hills, she was still the picture of a new Hampshire housewife. Grandpa Foster was equally impressive. Together, these stalwarts gave us the impression we were still in New England.

Several of the wives of homesteaders often helped out with housework at the ranch. Mrs. Ogden, a pretty blond woman, was in and out often with her two little girls. Her husband, Lou was a versatile man. He once gave me a great piece of advice. It was evening and he had come to fetch Mrs. Ogden home. I stood in the back doorway, waiting to close the door.

"Don't bother to lock that door, or in fact any doors or windows in your house, Mis' McCall. No one out in the ranch country would bother to steal any of your fine stuff." He paused to chuckle, then continued, "I bet you don't know what they *would* steal, though."

I gave up on this riddle and he went on to explain: "First of all, anything to do with horses: saddles, bridles, and such like. Next, anything to do with guns. Last comes a mighty important item. Can you guess what?" I shook my head.

That item, Mis' McCall, is *ready cash!*"

It was not long after this that Colonel William F. Hanley drove in from Harney County. Hal and I had met Colonel Hanley at the Corbetts' shortly after our arrival in Portland, and he had been the first person to give my sagging morale a boost. At the time, I was wearing a pink-and-white gingham dress under an expensive fur coat. Beaming at me as we shook hands, Mr.

Hanley exclaimed: *"Cali-ca! A pink cali-ca dress!* Now that's what I'd call the right kind of a girl."

In the early nineteen hundreds, W. F. Hanley, or "Colonel Bill," was one of the most colorful figures in Oregon. Looking like William Jennings Bryan, he dressed accordingly. His speech was picturesque. Dropping his "Gs" gave it an unusual charm. Later, after a second meeting in Prineville, Colonel Bill sent us a very fine letter. Written from one of his several southern Oregon ranches, on November 4, 1912, the letter went on in part:

> Dear Mr. and Mrs. McCall,
>
> Was sorry not to get a greater visit with you while in Prineville, but am coming back, and want to congratulate you on your stand of coming to Central Oregon and building such a well perfected home, fully intending to cast your lot with the people on the soil, for you will through your life be living with the real people of this country. . . .

The summer evening when Colonel Hanley finally drove into the ranch, Hal was at the gate to meet him. I was fairly bursting with excitement as the men came up on the porch. I called out:

"Oh, Colonel Hanley, what do you think? We are going to add some pigs to our livestock business, but people around here are giving us a great scare. They tell us coyotes will get the little pigs!"

Glancing at Hal, the kindly "Sage of Harney County" put his hand on my shoulder. "Girl," he said, "before you're through, *somethin'* will get *everythin' you've got!"* Together with Lou Ogden's words, how vividly in the following years of prosperity and depression did these words come back to me!

As time went on, many homesteaders gave up the unequal struggle and left, seeking "greener pastures." Today, however, many descendants of the remaining settlers have found success as a result of the endeavors of their sturdy forebears.

Other homesteaders who made a lasting impression on us were the Travis and the Evans families. Thomas Travis, a Chicago lawyer, had migrated to the West, seeking better health in virgin Oregon. He had taken up land to the east of our ranch. With the help of his attractive wife—a music teacher from Chicago—he built a comfortable house and an intricate system of ditches to water his dry, homestead acres. With his expert legal mind and fairly able body, he believed he could lick the arid acres; but the contest proved too great. Despite a lively business of her own with music pupils from the surrounding area, Mrs. Travis eventually became discouraged and left.

Alone, Travis tried to battle on. Finally realizing the futility of his efforts, he too left. Today, a few straggling, hand-built, broken dikes are mute witness to his defeat. . . .

> They crossed the final mountain in their path,
> A lofty rampart with a weathered peak,
> Like a forbidding god enthroned, whose wrath
> Would halt the timid and deter the weak.
> The two had come by perilous strands of road
> Festooned like cobwebs up the mountain side—
> He drove his own team in the country's mode,
> And she beside him but three days a bride.
> Hills beyond hills she saw, tier after tier,
> With desolate rounded crests as bare as a stone,
> And lost in this wild chaos, far or near,
> Were the few acres they would call their own. . .

> There was no water, but the soil was good,
> With sagebrush higher than a tall man's shoulder;
> Such land would make a farm if any would,
> And that, he said, before they were much older,
> She helped him build the shack beneath the hill—
> In her own way—for every flimsy rafter
> Went up, the doors were fitted, every sill
> Was nailed to snatches of song and laughter.
> He carted water, till the well was dug,
> From the warm spring three miles or more away. . .

They had their dreams of green alfalfa fields
With thriving growths to cut—and lusty clover.
Of yellow acres and their yellow yields
To fill their granaries and brim them over.
Seasons would follow—summer follow spring
As orderly as in a gentler place;
By sowing and by reaping they might bring
Time to a desert that had known but space. . .

Meanwhile he fenced, prepared the soil for seed—
He had that passion for the earth that spares
No pains—he laughed at toil—such was his breed—
In three years more the homestead would be theirs.
Urged by her love of home, with him to please,
She worked as early at her tasks, and late;
She helped him carry water for the trees,
And made a garden that the gophers ate. . . .

The wind blew dust to make her cleaning vain,
But never any downpour for the grain. . .

Disheartened neighbors vanished one by one,
She watched the sagebrush billow in the sun,
A lonelier exile on a lonelier shore.
Then life so long a tread of weariness
Waned suddenly, perhaps to her surprise,
And one blue-aproned, faded woman less
Stared from a door with hunger in her eyes. . .
And he surrendered what faith he had kept
To an empty kitchen and a hearth unswept.

Only a wall is left . . . the fallen frame
Lies like a bleached and scattered skeleton,
And they who thought to build and to reclaim
Are gone, as wilder tribes have come and gone.
With sun and wind across the burning sand,
The desert ruthlessly has taken all
That marked their brief intrusion save a strand
Of sagging fence, a reach of silvered wall.
Indifferent and timeless as the stars,

Few are the records it will not erase—
The futile footprints and the surfaced scars
Of men too puny for its light and space.
From age to age the waste shall brood and dream,
Mysterious and silent and supreme.*

Into the abandoned Travis house moved a family named Evans: mother, father, two boys, and four girls. Mrs. Evans, recently widowed, had remarried; and rumor had it that the present Mr. Evans was a very unstable character.

Hal and I knew little about these new neighbors until one spring evening when their twelve-year-old boy appeared at our back door. After giving his name, he asked Hal for work in the cow barn. There was always need of extra help in the cow barn, so the next day Hal put the boy, David Evans, to work. Everything went smoothly until one evening at supper when we were startled by loud calls from David:

"Mr. McCall! Mr. McCall! Come quick! Dad's going to kill us all!"

Hal jumped up from the table and hurried out.

Trailed by young David, he ran over to the bunkhouse. Joined by one of his men, he started off on foot for the Evans homestead. As they neared the house, Hal stopped and turned toward David:

"Look here, David, what's this all about?" Before the boy could answer, a bullet ricocheted off a nearby rock.

Quickly realizing the vulnerable position of all three, Hal said, "David, you will have to solve your own family problems . . . we have our own families to protect." With that, the two men tramped back to the ranch. As it turned out, Hal was right. The slightly deranged Mr. Evans had a habit of emphasizing his remarks by swinging a gun. Nothing serious so far had come from these senseless dramas.

*From the poem "Desert Wife" in *Desert Poems* by Ada Hasting Hedges. Published by the Metropolitan Press, 1930, Portland, Oregon.

Soon several more members of the Evans family found employment on our ranch; some in the dairy barn and others in the big house. Work in Hal's dairy proved to be a financial lifesaver for the Evans family, and for the time being, peace descended on the entire group.

Then, suddenly one morning, our entire household was awakened by shouts and the sound of thundering hooves. Hal rushed to a window where he was confronted by a scene worthy of Ben Hur. As in the chariot race, Mrs. Evans was standing upright on the front end of a cut-down buckboard, whip in hand, lashing wildly at the haunches of the Evans' only draft animal. Apparently she had reached the end of her rope and, terrified, was attempting to reach the county seat in Prineville for help. There she hoped to find restraint, by state authority, for her obviously deranged husband.

Unfortunately her hopes were dashed: following in hot pursuit came the enraged Evans himself. Before the woman could reach the river, she was overtaken by the galloping horse and rider.

After that, nothing significant occurred for about two months, when Mrs. Evans, Hal, and I drove into Prineville with a strong purpose. It was a hot summer afternoon. Earlier in the day, suspecting nothing, Evans himself had gone into Prineville. Knowing that her husband would be in town for some time, Mrs. Evans had sent David down to alert Hal to the fact that it would now be possible to have her husband picked up and placed in custodial care. On reaching Prineville, we signed commitment papers. Later that day he was picked up and taken to the State Hospital.

The following year, after a trip east to visit the family, we learned the latest of the Evans story. Frustrating his family's efforts, Evans had escaped from the State Hospital. Acquiring a small bit of property on the Idaho line, he built a portable shack. When law officers were closing in on him from Oregon, he shifted the shack into Idaho, and vice versa: when caught up with by the Idaho law, he rolled his shack back into Oregon.

Deranged Evans may have been, but the invention of the portable shack—balking all law officers' attempts to remove it—verged on genius.

8. Pendleton Round-Up—1913

It was late in January when Father sent us a carload of his fine stock from Dreamwold. As the train pulled into the little town of Redmond, word of the shipment got around the town like wildfire. It was a gray winter day but weather did not prevent the entire population from turning out for a street parade. The parade started from the railroad station. Out of the freight cars filed the animals "two by two." First came several registered Jersey heifers and a young Jersey bull. On their heels followed three of father's famous trotting mares and two stallions. For Daredevil, the old sire from Dreamwold, a black stallion, Father had paid $50,000. The horse was aging but Father hoped we would be able to raise some of his colts, crossing eastern and western stock. Prancing along beside him came the young black stallion, Dugal, known as Dug. Fine stock could be raised from him. After the horses came ewes and a ram. These were herded along by a couple of pedigreed Collie dogs. Bringing up the rear of the procession were fifty white Plymouth Rock hens with roosters, and fifty Rhode Island Red hens also with roosters.

As the fine eastern stock picked and pranced their way through the dirty snow and mud puddles in the town's little main street, the admiring crowd gave them a big hand. The spectacular showing turned that gray January day into an unusual holiday for Redmond. Its citizens had never before seen such a sight.

In February we started for Dreamwold, but before leaving

Hal gave strict instructions to the ranch foreman on caring for the valuable livestock. We were to make a quick trip east to keep a date with the stork and with Dr. George F. Washburn, the outstanding obstetrician at Massachusetts General Hospital— where Miss Haggart had trained. We didn't want to be gone long from the ranch and its new inhabitants.

However, we were at Dreamwold more than two months before "mother and nine-pound baby Tommy" were pronounced fit to travel. We were barely settled back on the ranch before Father, my brother, Doug, and my sisters, Marion and Bunny, arrived for a visit.

Both on the ranch and in the household, operations were running smoothly. Father and Doug were both enthusiastic over Oregon ranching prospects; but to my sister Marion, with her sharp business woman's mind, the merits needed pointing out. "I'd like to know more about running this ranch," she said one morning. "I'd like to be convinced that the cattle business is where you and Hal belong." I explained:

"Almost all our 640 acres are being put under irrigation. In the fall we're going to buy feeders—thin cattle, mostly steers. They'll be fattened up with the ranch crops, alfalfa and grain. In the spring, we'll market the then fat cattle at tremendous profit."

My sister looked at me in wonder, "Dote, how can you be all damn fool? If money were made as easily as that, the whole world would be out here in this corner of Oregon!"

My answer was simply, "Oh, Marion, where can we lose!" Not Marion but time gave the answer.

Later that summer we began to make plans for a trip to the famous Pendleton Roundup. Father was especially enthusiastic. Hal interviewed a number of drivers and checked cars with great care, finally settling on a large, roomy Chalmers automobile. Our chauffeur was to be a colorful but reliable ex-stage driver named Scotty. He had been chosen primarily because he swore he never touched a drop of liquor.

The morning we left, before we had even settled ourselves in the car, a family argument ensued among the six of us. Doug, who was casually swinging a revolver in and out of his holster, was asked by Hal to leave it behind. The majority of the party agreed, but there were so many pro and con arguments that everyone lost his enthusiasm about the trip—a bad start for so long a drive.

Knowing that the trip would take at least a day, or possibly a day and a night, we fortified ourselves with a large collection of books. Traveling through the grain country over bad roads, scraping the high centers and bouncing in deep ruts, the Chalmers had rough going. We had eight flat tires that first day. As each tire blew out, Scotty, a big, bluff man, reassured his disgruntled passengers that "the trouble will be fixed in no time. I don't need no help."

As Scotty was being well paid to deliver us to Pendleton, he "didn't get no help." Instead, we settled ourselves beside the road—as far apart from one another as possible—and opened our books, still seething with ill feeling. This rural public library group certainly made an unusual picture there in the sagebrush, miles from anywhere.

Before reaching Fossil, where we planned to break the dusty trip by having lunch, a really frightening grade loomed ahead of us. It wound up and up along the edge of a deep canyon. Father, who hated high places, ordered Scotty to stop the car: "Wait for me at the top of the grade." We all climbed out "to make the grade with him."

Scotty waited for us at the top, a broad smile on his face. As we started to pile back into the car, Father startled us by shouting, "My wallet, it's gone!" The family knew what that meant—the loss of more than $10,000. Father always carried ten $1,000 bills in that wallet, calling them his lucky pieces. Each one bore a story of some remarkable event, but most of them represented winning bets on his horses.

Scotty's smile grew broader. Holding out the missing wallet he said, "Here it is, Mr. Lawson, I found it on the seat when you got out." The honesty of that old ex-stage driver so impressed Father that he peeled off a $100 bill and handed it to Scotty. This put everyone in a gay mood. When we reached Fossil, the old hotel was a welcome sight. Father arranged for a room there where Marion, Bunny and I could wash off the two solid inches of desert dust covering us. In spite of our long linen dusters and heavy chiffon veiling over our hats, we were suffering from the effects of the choking dust of the road. Later, the tiny hotel's dining room was a short but welcome respite.

Scotty was waiting for us outside as we came from the dining room, but we were scarcely seated before the Chalmers shot out of Fossil like "a bat out of hell," as Father put it. Marion leaned over toward the front seat and said in a loud whisper:

"Father, this man has been drinking!"

"Oh, no," Father answered, "Scotty doesn't drink."

"Well, I guess I know whiskey when I smell it," came the heated reply. And we reeled on toward Pendleton, which we reached late that night—surprisingly all in one piece. After shedding our touring togs in the car, we parted with Scotty, whom we planned to meet the next morning.

The Pendleton Roundup—roundup in the raw at that time— is far famed for its colorful pageantry and daredevil exhibitions. But it was then in its infancy and was vastly different from the show of today. Many regulations and restrictions have gradually been introduced. The wild horse race was especially a massacre. Terrified animals, turned loose from their chutes, beat themselves to death against the ring's fences and railings. (Before we set off from the ranch, Hal had warned my sisters and me that any western rodeo was bound to be gory and brutal— far different horsemanship from what we had known in the East.)

As the cowboys finally caught their wild-horse victims and

58

struggled into the saddles, Hal turned to me, "Don't scream, don't start a fight and don't faint!" I suddenly remembered the comment of a Hay Creek neighbor, Sandy; it went something like this: "Western cowboys are the best riders and poorest horsemen in the world. They can ride anything with four legs, but they don't care if the animal dies right under them."

We were further appalled at the Indian women's race. As I remember, three of them were killed on opening day. We felt a little sick as we watched the shocking spectacle, but even sicker when the man next to me said, "What's the matter with you people? After all, they're only Indians!"

That evening we toured the Indian Village, and Father—who had been deeply touched by the tragic incidents—wanted to offer help in any way. It wasn't possible. The tepee village, on the outskirts of Pendleton, was not in mourning for its own lost tribeswomen. They were holding a ceremonial dance around a giant bonfire. Garbed in their vivid and magnificent regalia, with firelight flickering on their copper faces, these Indians etched a picture in my mind that I have never forgotten.

We stayed in Pendleton two days and nights, and counted on using the car and Scotty while there. However, our party caught a glimpse of the Chalmers only once, with a drunken Scotty at the wheel, his boon companions weaving and jumping, screaming and shrieking in the back seat. We gave up hope of ever catching our "non-drinking" ex-stage driver and came home by train.

Tom Sharp, driving home after the Roundup along the same road we had previously taken, saw Scotty briefly as the latter flew down that long, steep grade. He was dressed in Father's English black and white automobile coat and hat to match. As Scotty sped by, he leaned out of the car and, waving the hat, shouted,

"Say, Tom, do I look like *him*?"

9. The Horse Comes First

The Pendleton Roundup and its cowboys were a shock to us, although I had already begun to realize that the popular conception of the cowboy-hero was not true. However, when I was a girl in Boston, I had read stories by western writers and was brought up to see them more or less like Frederic Remington's statues and paintings. They were heroes. They loved their horses more than themselves, valued them, and kept them in fine condition.

Earlier, when Sandy made his remark about cowboys being "the best riders and the poorest horsemen in the world," I thought he might be slightly prejudiced, for there is an old slogan that goes: "To an Englishman his horse comes first, his dog second, his wife third."

Hal and I, fresh from the East and employing Westerners to work our stock, were beginning to see this unsavory side of the western cowboy-hero, but we continued to be horrified even after we had been some time in the West. There was a great contrast between the training of horses in the East and the training and breaking of horses in the West, for "breaking a horse," in western lingo was taken literally.

Our first trip to the Pendleton Roundup had been exciting but we were appalled at the cruelty, which was apparently ignored or condoned by both spectators and judges. However, during the following years, we saw many more instances of cowboy cruelty in rodeos both large and small.

When Father sent out the stock from Dreamwold, he included both racing mares and stallions. As it turned out, the old stallion, Daredevil, was too old for breeding, but we did raise many beautiful horses sired by Dugal. These were crossed with the western mares, the idea being that we would have the stability of the western horse plus the spirit and beauty of the hot-blooded stallion. We *expected* to find these virtues, but as it turned out, we found mostly vices. The colts, from crossbreeding, were beautiful black horses with white feet—"all fire and no sense." They proved very difficult to "break" at all.

One afternoon, in a more-or-less "gentle" roundup of some of our stock, a young filly, Black Skeeter, broke away and ran around the corner and up onto the rimrock. While two men with ropes followed her, she raced to the very edge of the rimrock. As the riders came nearer and nearer, the terrified horse, backing away, lost her footing and plunged over the edge of the rimrock. When the riders later found her, she was lying lifeless, with a broken neck.

> Gallop, gallop down the plain,
> Nostrils wide and tossing mane!
> Through the juniper, through the sage—
> Fleet and proud of your lineage.
> Sweep and plunge—around—around—
> Swifter, swifter drum the ground!
> Let your black sides reach for breath,
> Panting heart, you race with Death.
>
> You are lithe and you are strong—
> Rope is subtle, tight the thong.
> Never halt to gaze or wonder,
> Let your mad hoofs thunder, thunder!
> Slacken not your frenzied pace,
> For this, I fear, is your last race. . .*

*From the poem "Wild Stallion," in *Desert Poems* by Ada Hastings Hedges. Published by the Metropolitan Press, 1930, Portland, Oregon.

As Easterners coming into the Central Oregon country, we adjusted to many new things, but we never became accustomed to the harsh western treatment of horses. On the other hand, we were greatly impressed by the care and concern of western livestock breeders for their animals. Some stockmen showed even more concern for the welfare of their young stock than for the welfare of their own families!

At Dreamwold, stock breeding had been a taboo subject beyond the boundaries of the stables and barns. My sisters and I never knew where any of the actual breeding of our horses took place. I remember, though, one Sunday morning when we were driving over to the beach. As we crossed the railroad tracks, I noticed a groom leading my own bay mare out of one of Dreamwold's gates. I also saw another groom coming out a side road with a horse. In the background, I saw a small building constructed like all the other Dreamwold buildings, but I had never noticed it before. I asked Michael Kelly, our coachman, "What is that building, Michael? I never noticed it before. And why are the horses coming in and out?"

From my seat in the back of the carriage, I saw Michael's ears growing red as he answered, "Oh, you wouldn't be interested in that, Miss Dote."

Coming from such a sheltered background, it was difficult to re-adjust to the western frankness in stock breeding. The first time that big Jim West came spanking down Crooked River in a light sulky driving his Percheron stallion, I was wholly unaware of his mission.

Later that day, Hal explained, "In the vernacular of stock breeding, Dote, that big old fellow, Jim West, stands a stallion. I know that you don't understand what I'm talking about but I'll try to explain. We ranchers have work horses. As you know, it takes a great many to put up the crops. To make our business pay, the mares must have foals. To all and sundry, Jim West's

Percheron is known as "Big Daddy," and the results of his visits are much the same as that of the stork's."

As Hal went on talking, I did begin to understand. One thing that became very clear to me almost immediately was why Michael's ears had turned red that day in the carriage. Gradually I became accustomed to Jim West's visits—but not so my sister Marion. On one of Jim West's "dates" at the ranch, Marion happened to be staying with us. As usual, his arrival created considerable excitement. Marion strongly disapproved of any type of lusty, rugged life in either animals or people, and her reaction that day very nearly closed down our livestock business.

She came flying onto the porch where Miss Haggart and I were sitting. Ordinarily, Marion was considered a great beauty, with naturally wavy, dark brown hair and deep blue eyes. But that day she was flushed with anger and indignation. She demanded: "For heaven's sake, Dorothy, will you go over to that corral and stop all that disgusting commotion. It is indecent and outrageous!"

I had come, by that time, a long way from Boston in my understanding of the reality of stock breeding. I simply couldn't believe she was serious.

"No, Marion, I can't do that, for if it were not for all that 'commotion' in the corral, we would not be in the livestock business today."

10. The Pig Story

In the spring of 1914, we made a now traditional trip back to Dreamwold. There, on a lovely April morning, little Dorothy McCall came into the world. Her two small brothers had been left with Miss Haggart in a cottage at Mrs. Howe's in Hood River.

The baby's trip back to Oregon was epic. My aunt and my father and my father's handsome English secretary, Miller, traveled back with the baby girl and me. We stopped at Hood River to pick up Miss Haggart and the boys; and as usual, we broke the long train trip with a stay there of several days.

During our stay, a well-known newspaperman, Fred Lockley, representing the *Oregon Journal,* came up to interview my Father. Mr. Lockley was interested in his opinions on the stockmarket crisis. (An Austrian archduke had been assassinated and World War I was imminent.) Father, however, jovially evaded business issues. Pointing at the baby basket he answered Mr. Lockley,

"See that basket over there? You are looking at the most famous basket in Oregon. Every year it goes back to Boston empty, and comes back to Oregon with a new citizen."

Since Father planned to stay several months with us, Miller had been brought along to keep him in touch with his Boston office through correspondence and long-distance telephone calls. Meantime, the stock market veered up and down, mostly down, but telegrams and emissaries to the ranch made no impression on Father. He had made up his mind. Stock markets would be forgotten while he enjoyed himself with his grandchildren.

Father settled on the ranch for the better part of that year. Together, he and Hal supervised the development of the newly acquired 160 acres adjoining our property to the east. Land was leveled, buildings started, and an efficient irrigation system laid out.

Shortly after, despite Hal's opposition, Father embarked on his newest enterprise—the raising of pure-bred hogs. Since coming west the first time, he had become intensely interested in pigs; he had never before seen these animals in green alfalfa fields.

About this time, in the spring of 1914, additional members of both families arrived for a look at the Great Northwest. Sisters, brothers, and friends from the East came swarming out to the ranch. Among these visitors was my younger brother, Doug, who immediately caught "pig fever"; he became fascinated with Father's idea of establishing a new strain. Whenever Father launched a new project, he did it in a grand manner, and there was nothing conservative about his ideas or his methods of developing them.

Hal was still trying to sell him on the advantages of cattle over pigs when Doug arrived. Added to his belief in cattle, Hal had a particular antipathy to pigs; but in spite of all Hal's arguments, Father's answer was still the same:

"It takes a cow nine months to have a calf. How many times a year do pigs farrow? I want action, Hal." And action was what he got. Scores of letters were dictated to Miller, whose secretarial duties quickly doubled. In the short time Miller had been on the ranch, he had learned to ride a horse and was gradually adjusting to the ways of the West. Despite his strong English accent, he had become very popular with the neighbors, but with Father's new project, he suddenly had time for little else.

It was not long before the results of Father's labors began pouring into the ranch. Eventually six different breeds of hogs arrived to be housed and provided for temporarily. They were magnificent stock. The best of every breed was represented. There were Chester Whites, black Poland Chinas, and brown Duroc-Jerseys, shipped from outstanding breeders all over the country.

Because Father was determined to get started right away, hogs began arriving before the necessary equipment. This was the first mistake: there was no place to house the early arrivals. Proper shelter is a very important part of successful hog raising. No livestock requires better protection. Under construction at the upper ranch was a modern building to house the pigs, where eventually they would be comfortably settled. The pens in the buildings had to be roomy so that at farrowing time, there would be no danger of the sow rolling on the baby pigs. Temporarily the hogs were housed in individual six-foot galvanized tin houses.

There was great excitement with the arrival of the first sow, and from then on the excitement mounted. With the subsequent arrival of more sows and boars, the pig population exploded; but the inadequate housing brought about a grim situation. Hal's forebodings began to be realized, for as a result of farrowing in cramped quarters, the mortality rate of the piglets increased.

Miller was delegated to keep the records; he became secretary to the pigs as well as to Father. One of his duties was to bring a daily report from the foreman of the pig operation to Father. Early in the morning, he would check at each maternity ward. As Miller knocked on Father's door to submit the report, the rest of us would tiptoe to the foot of the stairs and listen. At the start of the pig venture, the message was usually grim:

"Mr. Lawson, Bonny B. farrowed last night. There are only two pigs left of the litter. Three were squashed and two eaten." Then there was Lilly Belle, a huge white sow: "None of Lilly Belle's pigs survived." And so it went down through the long-legged Yorkshires, the Tamworths, the black Poland Chinas, and the handsome white-belted Hampshires.

Disgusted, Father would pull down the shades and go back to sleep. We could always tell the tide of the current pig population—whether it was running high or low—just by the set of the window shades!

As time went on and new equipment arrived, the situation adjusted itself. Properly housed, the big sows were able to raise their piglets. Eventually, the large buildings were completed on the upper ranch and the pigs were moved into spacious surroundings. The hog barn was 800 feet long, airy, sturdy, and well equipped to provide the most excellent accommodations for production. But it was a case of too much, too late.

Not all the project, however, was disastrous. There were high spots. One of the happiest notes on the pig venture was the sturdiness and endurance of the Hampshires. Many of the young stock attained maturity while my Father was still at the ranch. They appealed to this flamboyant man, and he had two particular pets. We called them "the girls," but their real names were more impressive. Father dubbed them Arabella and Cinderella. Every morning Arabella and Cinderella would somehow escape from their quarters and come strolling over the ditch.

Pushing the gate open with their snouts, they would meander over the lawn to Father's window. With squeals and grunts, they would try to summon him to the window. Before Father appeared, the racket would have attracted everyone in the house— but "the girls" refused to settle for any of the rest of us.

Finally, Father's window would bang open and he would appear with a gay, "Good morning, girls," and toss them an apple or carrot. Mission accomplished, the two "girls" would amble back to their quarters.

By spring, 1915—before he had realized any financial returns on the pig project—Father began to receive urgent messages from the East; he must return immediately to Boston. But he was having a marvelous time; it was the first really relaxed, happy time since my mother's death nine years earlier. The lack of material returns on his investment he seemed to regard as incidental. My usually fastidious father often rode on the wagon when one of the men was hauling gravel for the developing upper ranch. One morning as he and one of the men were starting out, Miller came rushing after them:

"Mr. Lawson, Mr. Lawson," he shouted, "New York is calling!" Father scrambled off the wagon and hurried back to the house. Later, when Fred came back, Father was waiting for him at the gate.

"Mr. Lawson," Fred apologized, "I hope that call didn't lose you any money."

"Lose me any money, Fred?" Father laughed and added, "Why, I just made another million!"

One of the men on the ranch, a little Irishman, was so dedicated to the pig-breeding project that he practically lived with the animals. Though his real name was Tommy Cronin, we had dubbed him Tommy Pig. One day, Hal came into the house, calling to me,

"Will you please come and do something with Tommy Pig's hand, Dote?" He was closely followed by Tommy Pig himself, who smilingly held out his left hand. I was speechless. The whole hand, starting from an infected cut below his thumb, had swelled and an angry red streak was beginning to run up his arm. Hal explained,

"I've tried and tried to get him to go to the doctor, even warning him that he may lose his arm, but he just tells me, 'No, no, I'm not going to any doctor. He'll just charge me ten dollars. I bet Mis' McCall can do just as good a job for me, and she won't charge me nothin' for it.'" Tommy was noted for his frugal spending.

From Boston, we had brought with us a well-equipped medicine chest, including several tall bottles of Cabot's Sulpho-

Naphthol—a powerful sheep-dip kind of disinfectant—and a rattlesnake kit. These remedies had more than once saved us in an emergency. We had become well experienced in "country doctoring."

I beckoned Tommy into the laundry room, and Hal brought in a large bucket of hot water into which he dumped a generous splash of Sulpho-Naphthol. Handing me a bottle of his best Canadian Rye whiskey, Hal said, "If he starts to faint, shove this down his throat." With that bit of sage advice, he returned to his ranch chores.

Holding Tommy's outstretched left arm, I plunged a sterilized knife into his red, swollen hand, then quickly dropped his hand into the bucket of hot solution. As the disinfectant hit the open wound, Tommy Pig turned pea-green. Grabbing the bottle of rye whiskey, I shoved it into his mouth and told him to swallow.

After several gulps, his color began to come back, and the little Irishman, with a bright gleam in his eyes, held out his right hand.

"Say, Mis' McCall, here's my other hand. If you'll give me another swig of that rye whiskey, you can cut this one too!"

As the pig drama unfolded, Doug gradually became interested in the project; so interested, in fact, that he started a project of his own. His "plant" was across the river in the willows. Here he kept several sows. Of course, Father thought that Doug's "plant" was just a passing fancy—as being midwife to pigs was quite a switch from the football field of Harvard College. Finally, though, he began to take his son seriously when he realized that Doug was spending most of his time with the sows, especially at farrowing time. Under Doug's tender care, the newborn piglets thrived. In good weather or bad, expectant sows were served their boiling water several times a day. Sometimes Doug wouldn't come home until midnight, then would leave at the crack of dawn, depending on what was going on in the maternity ward. He gave up shaving, grew a beard, and went around looking like some ruffian in a western movie.

In the midst of all this, an emissary arrived from the East. It was my older brother Arnold, who had come in person to drag Father back to his business in Boston. When the telegram came, advising us of his arrival, Doug hurried over to Redmond to meet him. Arnold—who had spent much of his life in England— stepped out onto the Redmond station platform in clothes fresh from London: topcoat, derby hat, and cane. His brother Doug clambered up the steps of the platform, still wearing his "maternity outfit": battered sombrero, muddy boots, and whiskers. Grabbing Arnold by his immaculate English sleeve, Doug muttered, "For God's sake, swallow that cane or they'll lynch you out here!"

After the initial shock, Arnold stayed two weeks at the ranch. He was a great horseman and outdoor man—this side of the ranch appealed to him. But he disliked the isolation and the necessity of a daily routine. As an "emissary" he was a failure for he went back to Boston alone. Father was currently more absorbed in the western stock than the eastern stock market.

11. Murder on Crooked River

Even though Arnold had gone back to Boston alone, his trip eventually brought results: Father began to realize the time had come for him to get back to his office on State Street. He had had his wonderful year on the ranch. Though we were all disappointed, we realized this was a right decision.

While making plans for his trip, Father—who was greatly impressed by Doug's interest in ranching—decided to buy him a place of his own. My brother was delighted and he and Hal immediately started looking at ranches.

The news that millionaire money was loose in Central Oregon spread like wildfire. Potential sellers swarmed out to our ranch. One of the most prominent of these was Charles Colby, a big, cadaverous man whose unsavory reputation was common talk on Prineville streets. Colby was anxious to sell his place and move away, and this looked like a chance to sell and clear out. It was rumored that he had killed several men in Montana before coming to Oregon; also that he could solve the riddle of peddler Shorty Davis's mysterious disappearance. Circumstantial evidence indicated that Davis was last seen dickering with Charlie Colby, who was renowned for his violent temper. His horse and peddler's wagon were found, but from that time on, never a trace of Shorty Davis.

Hal and I had met Colby some two years before, when tales had reached his ears that a wealthy young couple from the East were eager to establish themselves in the fertile West. Then also he had been looking for an opportunity to sell his holdings and get out. . . On that first visit, Hal and I were getting ready to trim the Christmas tree when Colby came riding in from his ranch above Prineville. Hal went out to meet him at the back gate and brought him into the living room. We were both impressed with the friendliness of the man. We had coffee and he gave us a glowing description of Mrs. Colby. At that time, he must have been sixty years old and she in her early thirties. (Later on, when we finally met Mrs. Colby, we were even more puzzled at the strange affiliation. She was a lovely young woman and seemed very fond of "her Charlie." During subsequent visits, we were even more mystified for, along with her good looks, she was a fine cook and housewife.)

On that particular Christmas Eve, after the men had talked awhile and Hal had gone out to the barn, Colby stayed. I was surprised when he suggested that he would help trim the tree. I was even more surprised to see how deftly he handled the fragile Christmas ornaments. When I commented on this, he seemed pleased, then offered to tell me a bit about his childhood. It was a tragic story: orphaned at the age of nine, he had started out on his own, sleeping under culverts and in haystacks. Somehow he had managed to survive, but the effort had turned him into a hardened, embittered man.

It was getting late when we finished talking. We sat without speaking for several minutes. Suddenly into my mind came the chilling realization that little Harry and I were alone in the empty, shadowy house with the notorious Charlie Colby! It was an uneasy feeling, for the story of his strange, grim childhood, added to what I already knew of his reputation, was far from reassuring. Quickly I suggested we go on with the tree.

Later, when Hal came in from the barn, he was surprised to see Colby teetering on the trimming stool, reaching for the top of the tree. After tenderly placing a silver star on the highest branch, he stepped down and turned to us.

"Well, folks, what do you think of it?"

Hal looked at me in amazement. I was scarcely less surprised. Tenderness! In the rumored killer, Charlie Colby?

Rather shakily I answered, "It's perfect, Mr. Colby. I hope you'll always be around to trim our Christmas trees with us." A few minutes later, Charlie Colby, wishing us well, was on his way home.

Now, some two years later, it was a different Colby from the friendly man who had last left the ranch with Christmas in his heart, wishing us well. When Colby came riding in that day, I met him at the back gate as the men were all away.

"It's nice to see you again, Mr. Colby." Surprised at his stern demeanor, I added, "I'm only sorry you didn't bring Mrs. Colby with you." There was not a sign of warmth in the somber man staring at me from his horse.

"I came to see the men, Mrs. McCall. I hear your father is buying a ranch for your brother, and am sure that my ranch will exactly fit the bill." Nervous about inviting him into the house, I hastily said, "I would ask you in, but your business is strictly with the men. All three of them are away until late this evening. Should I give them the message?"

"Just tell 'em, Mis' McCall, to come on over to the ranch tomorrow. I'll be there all day." With these words he wheeled his horse around and galloped off.

The following day, Doug and Hal went over to see the Colby place, and for a while it seemed to be the best buy of all. Before making the final choice, though, they also looked over several other ranches. In the final decision, the Colby place was ruled out. Father signed papers for a ranch above Prineville before he and Doug took off for Boston.

When news of the sale reached Colby, he was furious. His creditors were closing in on him and his wife was threatening to leave him. In a telephone call, he warned Hal that unless Father and Doug came back and canceled their deal on the other ranch, he would come out and settle with Hal.

I was awfully worried that morning but Hal said to me, "Don't worry. Colby's just talking big." I merely asked, "What happened to Shorty Davis?"

Several mornings later, we had another telephone call from Mr. Colby. He was exceedingly grim and explained to Hal that he had many debts and was counting heavily on the ranch deal going through. Under these circumstances, he was ready to use violent means to hold what he had left. He gave Hal two alternatives: either bring Doug or my father back from Boston to draw up papers, or face the deadly consequences!

Hal said, "Oh, come off it, Charlie. You know I can't bring my brother-in-law or Mrs. McCall's father back from Boston. I'll do anything I can to help you, but the ranch deal is definitely off." On this final note, Colby went berserk. Shouting at Hal that he would be out within the hour, he slammed the receiver down.

All this happened on a peaceful, sunny morning. Even with Colby's killer reputation, murder just didn't seem real. "I'm going on down to meet him at the river, Dote," Hal said. After he started, I tagged along behind, watching from the willows as Hal neared the ford. Then I saw Colby on his big black horse, riding toward the river. When he reached the ford, Hal, seeing him, called out, "Come on over, Charlie."

Completely taken by surprise at the friendly greeting, Colby reined in his horse, his hand on his gun. Again Hal called out, "Come on, Charlie, let's talk this thing over!"

Taking his hand off his gun, Colby turned and, without a word, headed his horse toward town. Straight through Prineville he thundered, murder in his heart, on up Crooked River to the ranch where his devoted wife was waiting for him at the gate. Jerking his spent and sweating horse to a halt, he answered her glad cry of "Charlie!" with a single shot. The crack of a second report brought to a close the explosive and tormented existence of Charlie Colby.

12. The Gay Days

During this time, we were caught up on the crest of a wave of success; we were on Easy Street. Money began talking to money and fun-loving, gay days followed.

A young bachelor, John T. "Spokes" Wheeler, an insurance man from the East who had already settled in Prineville, became the foremost booster for land sales in our part of the country. On a return trip to Oregon from the East, Spokes met a young man from New York, fresh out of Yale. The young man was on his way to San Francisco. At breakfast the following morning, Spokes, an avid salesman, discovered the identity of his new friend—he was a member of an outstanding New York family.

At that time, Sunday supplements of newspapers, both in the East and in the West, were publishing banner headlines over stories of college boys on the eastern Gold Coast being snatched up by girl "gold diggers" patrolling that coast. And "Gold Coast" boys were gullible prey for determined ladies on the prowl. The young man from Yale and another college boy had been caught up by two of these young "gold diggers." Both boys had fled New York. One had reached San Francisco safely and was there waiting for the arrival of the other—Spokes' new friend. By the time he got off the train, Spokes had convinced the young man that Central Oregon would be the best place for locating. A visit in the West was arranged after the San Francisco reunion.

When Spokes later visited us, he was enthusiastic over his latest "find," and special entertainment was planned at the ranch to celebrate the arrival of the Yale man. A lovely, eligible young lady from Portland was invited to be a house guest for the event. But, by the end of a week, with no word from San Francisco, the young lady had become restless. Though apprehensive, Hal and I tried to be reassuring: "Don't be discouraged and give up and go home, that fellow may come walking in here any minute."

One morning shortly thereafter, the telephone rang; it was a message from our man in San Francisco: "Sorry, unavoidably detained in San Francisco. Am writing." Before any further word came, Sunday papers reached the ranch. Headlines described the story of the two young men from New York. Fleeing to the West Coast, they had been hotly pursued across the country by the determined "gold diggers," overtaken, and married in San Francisco.

One couple returned to New York to face the angry parents, but the other couple—the young man from Yale with his victorious bride—decided to take their chances in the West. A second telegram from California advised Spokes that they planned to settle in Prineville and were in the market for a cattle ranch.

Spokes, the avid salesman, was ecstatic, but great gloom descended on the rest of us: seemingly heartbroken, our disillusioned house guest packed and left for Portland.

Soon the newlyweds arrived in Prineville, where they were met by a beaming Spokes Wheeler, eager to put through an immediate land deal. They were temporarily settled in the old Prineville Hotel and, on the following day, were taken on an extensive tour of available ranch properties.

A number of sophisticated young people from the East, many of them married couples, had already settled on ranches around Prineville, and their enthusiasm to tackle life in the raw was boundless. Their developed ranches greatly impressed our new arrivals, and it was not long before papers were drawn up and signed. Even Spokes himself was amazed at the speed with which the deal went through.

The gay days continued from 1914 until we entered the war in 1917. During this period the old Prineville Hotel was the center of much activity, both political and social, and it served as a private club for prominent local citizens. The owner and operator, Mrs. MacDowell, an astute business woman, always had a hearty welcome for her prosperous guests. The main street on which the two-storied structure stood was typically western, dusty and drab, but the hotel's linoleum floors were spotless. The excitement-seeking eastern imports spent as much time dancing on the dining room linoleum as they did working their irrigation ditches.

When Doug came back from Boston he was a welcome addition to the group. Within a short time he organized them into an amateur dramatic club which was to tour the surrounding countryside over the next few years. They hauled their own scenery in a truck and traveled on horseback between the towns. The night they staged "Northern Lights" in Madras, one of the players was shot in the rear. The prop man had forgotten to insert blank cartridges in one of the loaded guns.

Horrified, a member of the company called out the proverbial question, "Is there a doctor in the house?" This was greeted by roars of laughter. It proved impossible to convince anyone in the audience that a serious accident had occurred until the victim was carried backstage, leaving a trail of blood. He was not seen in the saddle for many months.

The miscellany of buildings they performed in often required athletic prowess. When a scene called for an actor a make a "stage exit" from one wing and his reappearance from the opposite wing, he would have to circle the building to accomplish this. Crises were common as the actors became entangled in barbed wire fences, or fell over obstructions and various hurdles in the black of night. One night as a player ran the obstacle course, he became hooked on a barbed wire fence and his fellow actor was forced to ad lib until he reappeared in another pair of trousers.

Doug came back from these week-end tours full of tales of the company's exploits. "You were right, Hal," my spirited brother would say, "there's no place like the West."

We had many spirited arguments before Father left for the East. Hal and I were surprised one morning to see a shiny new Buick at the gate. We both thought more friends had arrived unexpectedly, but neither of us recognized the car. From a bedroom window, Father called to me, "How do you like it, Dote?" Puzzled, I went out to have a closer look and saw, on the door, the initials "DLM". Just then, Hal appeared on the scene.

"What's this all about? Seems you've got a new car!"

With Father still at the window, I answered, "Oh, isn't it beautiful, Hal. The sad part of it is, I don't think we can keep it."

"What's your idea, Dote?"

"If we keep this fancy little Buick, we'll be just too popular. The ranch will go down the drain while we are touring friends all around the country." Hal immediately got the idea.

When Father finally came downstairs, he was indignant.

"Now, what's the problem; don't either of you want to get in and take a ride?"

Not wanting to hurt him or seem unreasonable, Hal jumped into the gap. "Would it be possible, Mr. Lawson, to trade this in on a Buick truck? It's the one thing we need more than anything else on the ranch."

At first, Father was heartbroken. He wanted a glamorous car for his glamorous daughter, but now the daughter wanted a truck!

As Hal went on to explain, it didn't take long for Father to understand our problem and he finally agreed to the deal. Just before Father left, a Buick truck was delivered at our back gate.

Before leaving for Boston with Father, Doug had disposed of his pig stock. His newly acquired ranch up Crooked River was to be equipped with Percheron Horses, but another argument came up on the subject of stock before they left.

"Why not cattle, Mr. Lawson?" Hal asked. "After all, this is cattle country and Doug might as well make money on his investment."

As usual, Father was adamant. "You have cattle, Hal. Let's have my money go into something different for Doug: horses—Percherons." So Percherons it was. Doug started out with a thriving business on his upper Crooked River ranch.

Besides the breeding stock of heavy horses, one of Doug's most prized possessions was a sorrel saddle horse called Tufty. While a colt, Tufty had been trained by our old foreman, Roy Rannells, who always maintained that Tufty was the fastest little horse in any part of the country.

One late afternoon while driving our cattle above Bend to summer pasture, Doug became separated from the rest of the riders and lost his way. Toward dark, he came upon an isolated eating place far from the traveled road. While munching a sandwich there, he noticed two of the most evil-looking characters he'd ever seen, over in a dim corner. They were eyeing him with more than an ordinary interest and he figured they had picked him out as easy prey. Even in his western clothes, he looked to them like a moneyed dude from the East.

Instinct can be a great protector. Doug got up and sauntered toward the men's room; in those days an outside privy. Once through the doorway, he made a flying leap onto the waiting Tufty's back. At the touch of the unfamiliar spur, the sorrel horse flattened out and broke all records into the town of Bend.

A final note on Tufty: Doug left him on his ranch when he went away to war. A short while later, Hal was notified by the caretakers that Tufty had died. Hal immediately went up to the ranch but found no trace of the dead horse. He figured that the fast little horse had probably been sold to racetrack operators.

Years later, at races in Tygh Valley, Roy Rannells noticed an old sorrel nag running in one of them. He seemed nearly winded. Into Roy's mind flashed, "Skinny and old, that sorrel still looks like Tufty!" After the race, Roy ran over to the fence and, snapping his fingers, called out,

"Tufty! Hi, Tufty!" Automatically the old horse responded to that familiar call and gesture. He shakily rose on his hind legs and began to paw the air. As Roy leaped over the fence, the old sorrel crashed to the ground.

When Roy later told us the story, with tears in his eyes, he added, "That was valiant old Tufty's last performance."

When Doug's ranch house was nearing completion, we started making frequent excursions there—twenty miles east of Prineville. Doug had many friends who wanted to help with the decoration. It was then that the Buick truck really came into its own. Planks were placed across the back and with this makeshift arrangement we could transport twelve or fourteen people. It seemed everyone was ready to pitch in and help. So Father really had the last laugh! If we had kept the dinky little Buick, seating five passengers, we would have never had the problems of the over-loaded truck.

Both Hal and I loved outdoor life, enjoyed people, and an occasional party, but gradually it became necessary for us to give up a good many of the group gaieties. The development of the ranch and raising our small children demanded more and more of our time.

It was not only the local people who provided excitement, there were others from "over the mountains."

When stockmen went down to Portland on cattle business, they usually stayed at the Imperial Hotel, but when excitement-seeking ranchers went down to the city on week-ends, they would put up at the Benson Hotel. Through hunting and fishing season, the tide turned: visitors from the "big city" poured into Central Oregon. Despite our increasing responsibilities, Hal and I would join the latter group on special occasions.

About this time, there was a great influx of people we had known from Portland, Philadelphia, and New York, who were buying up property along the Metolius River and around Sisters, Oregon. These people were going in for sheep ranching in a big way. The tiny town of Sisters to the west of us became a polo and horse-racing center. On week-ends, Portlanders often brought up ponies and race horses.

Headquarters was always the Bailey ranch, where hospitality was fabulous. Gourmet lamb dinners were the order of the day and no one who had eaten one would ever forget it. Meredith Bailey, with his young wife, had come out from Philadelphia and bought a sheep ranch. Meredith's younger brother, Curtis, was one of the gay, eligible young bachelors. Ben Tone (Bernard L. Tone from New York) "bached" with Curtis and they were in constant demand by the transplanted Easterners entertaining young ladies from home. When my sister, Bunny, and her friends came to spend vacations on the ranch, Hal and I relied heavily on Curtis and Ben to entertain them.

On one such vacation trip, Bunny brought with her a close friend from Boston, just returned from England. The night Hal met them at the train in Redmond, both girls were wildly excited over "the handsomest cowboy!" Apparently, both of them had devoted much of their time on the train to admiring a young man vividly described as "tall and curly-haired, with a dazzling smile and a ten-gallon hat." The hat made him a cowboy!

They pleaded with Hal to do some detective work on the stranger; they "just had to meet him." Laughingly, Hal came up with distressing information: the handsome "cowboy" was none other than George Palmer Putnam, very much married, mayor of Bend, and editor of the Bend newspaper. (In later years, the

Putnams were divorced and, in 1931, George Putnam became the husband of Amelia Earhart, the great aviatrix and the first woman to cross the Atlantic Ocean in an airplane.)

13. Civet Cats and Rattlesnakes

People in Central Oregon were just beginning to raise turkeys. At this time, I had a flourishing business with my white Plymouth Rock and Rhode Island Red chickens. Now, in a small way, I decided to try my luck with turkeys.

Among the original buildings on the ranch was the "world's most modern hen house." I had separated the two poultry breeds into two sections of the building with a third section reserved for a start of turkeys. Small wooden houses had been built for the hens with newly hatched chickens.

Into the midst of this activity arrived an old school friend of mine, Gertrude Cooper from Boston. Having known me since childhood and in a setting so completely opposite to my present one, Gertie was aghast at the boundless enthusiasm and energy I was pouring into my rapidly increasing chicken industry. The day after she arrived, I took her out to the hen house to show her this thriving poultry business. The night before, in one of the small chicken houses, there had been ten chicks with a large Plymouth Rock mother.

"Close your eyes, Gertie," I said. "When you see what I have here, I think you'll want to go into the chicken business with me." Gertie watched closely as I cautiously lifted the little wooden hen house. There sat the big, white, fluffy Plymouth Rock hen—not a sign of a chick! Puzzled, I picked up the hen.

Still no sign of a chick—not even a toenail! All chicks had vanished into thin air. Beside me I heard a caustic comment:

"Perhaps you *need* me in the chicken business, Dote!"

For several days this was a baffling mystery. Then came the morning we stepped into the big hen house where ten beautiful Rhode Island Red pullets were being groomed for the forthcoming county fair. They were all huddled in one dark corner in sinister silence. Cautiously tiptoeing over to the corner, I picked up one of the pullets—pullets without heads! In horror, I dropped the mangled bird back on its massacred companions and ran out of the hen house.

The next morning I had another shock. In section 3 of the hen house, the board floor had some cracks. A turkey hen with a large brood was housed in this section. Usually the little turkeys would start flapping around when I came into the house: but on this morning, there was an ominous air about the place. The little turkeys couldn't move because each one had lost a leg. This did it! All worked stopped on the ranch and the men started an investigation immediately. They soon made a discovery: leading down from the rimrock at the back of the hen house was a narrow, well-worn path that continued on under the building. The floor boards were taken up and underneath was revealed a runway strewn with feathers and poultry bones. Traps were set and the floor boards replaced. With this method, we finally snared thirty-one civet cats under the floor of the hen house.

During the operation, I met my first civet cat face to face. One sunny morning, I was talking to a neighbor in front of the house. A snowy-white Plymouth Rock pullet came picking and pecking her way toward me. Suddenly the pullet stopped and reached under the house to peck.

As we stood chatting, I noticed that the pullet was no longer moving. Picking her up by the leg, I found myself holding a completely headless chicken! Speechless, I stared at a hole under the hen house. A small, malevolent face with steely, murderous eyes, stared back at me.

A civet cat is a small, long-bodied, and short-legged animal built like a weasel. His diminutive size makes him as deadly as the weasel for he can squeeze through as small an opening as that vicious animal. He also has the added protection of the skunk, with his power of emitting a strong and offensive odor in times of danger or attack. I was learning that you had to be rugged to survive all the exposures to the natural hazards of that primitive outdoor world. We were always dealing with the unexpected or unknown.

One of the deadliest threats was the rattlesnake. I had been told when we first settled in the country that it was one's duty to kill a rattler. The small children were alerted to run and scream whenever they saw a snake. Back in Massachusetts, I had always had a healthy fear of even a small garter snake. I would run in terror at the sight of the smallest one.

One sunny morning, I was sitting on the hot stone of the front porch drying my hair. My hair was long and made a kind of curtain over my eyes. Through the open French doors, I could hear Auntie, Hal, and Miss Haggart talking in the living room. In the process of drying my hair, I tossed it back from my face. Coiled up comfortably beside me and apparently sleeping, was the largest snake I had ever seen outside a zoo or a circus.

Fearing I might waken the sleeper and he would strike, I whispered loudly, "There's a great big snake out here beside me!" No answer came from the living room, so I spoke out!

"There's a great big snake out here beside me." Still no answer. In desperation, I jumped up screaming:

"For heaven's sake, come out here and kill this snake!" At that, Hal rushed through the doorway, then burst out laughing.

"That snake, Dote, you're so afraid of there on the step is one of the greatest assets to the farmer. It's a kindly snake, called a bull snake. It destroys gophers and field mice. Please remember that it is *not* a rattlesnake!"

Eventually I was to learn more about snakes and the law of the ranch land. That law demanded a concerted effort and continued determination to wage war on the "killer" rattlesnake. One must never stop fighting him. Among the rattlesnake's worst enemies is the collie dog. On one very hot morning, while Hal and I were talking at the back gate, our collie, Cim, came running down the road toward us. Suddenly he stopped. A coiled rattler was lying in the bright sun on the roadway. Cautiously Cim drew near the rattler. Then began a dance in the sunshine that would have won applause for a ballerina. On tiptoe, the dog swiftly started circling the snake and every so often dashed in, as the snake, open-mouthed, fangs exposed, struck back. Between strikes, as the snake's head followed the dog's movements, his slender, darting tongue had a hypnotic effect on us. But the collie was too quick for him. He was also having great fun, for he knew when and how to come in for the kill.

As we watched, fascinated, the dog waited for the precise moment when he could close in and grab the rattler at the back of the head. Suddenly he tossed the snake high into the air. He then trotted smugly over to us, knowing he had put on a great show. Back of him lay the still-twitching body of the dying rattlesnake.

Later on that year a rattler met its match in big Bill McDonald. Big Bill, who had extensive ranch operations, was out checking on his herd of sheep feeding on our land, and Hal was with him. While they were talking down in the field by the butte, Hal noticed a rattlesnake coiled near MacDonald's foot. In shifting his position, the big sheep man, who was wearing high, heavy leather boots, accidentally stepped on the rattler which instantly hissed, uncoiled, and struck at the leather leg. This byplay went unnoticed by Bill, who was deaf and kept right on talking. Hal, horrified, tried to interrupt, to make the man understand that he was in danger. Pointing to Big Bill's boot, Hal shouted, but to no avail. By this time the snake was hanging on the boot and striking again and again. Finally, Big Bill seemed to realize that Hal was paying little attention to his talk of sheep; seemingly he had been mesmerized by his own stories. Suddenly looking down at his boot, he saw the snake. Seeing the snake hanging from his boot, Bill McDonald burst into a loud guffaw. He patted Hal reassuringly on the shoulder and made his famous declaration:

"Oh, hell, Hal, them things won't hurt ya!"

14. Calamities Come in Threes

We were looking forward to a reunion at Dreamwold during the Christmas holidays of 1916. We tried to talk Doug into coming back with us, but he was too happy with his ranch and his many friends. All arrangements had been made for the trip; the house was ready to close, furniture was covered with sheets, and the two maids had been promised an extended Christmas vacation. The day before we were to leave, a telegram came saying that Hal's father, Governor-elect Samuel W. McCall of Massachusetts was enroute to the ranch for a brief visit.

The news completely disrupted our plans. The maids canceled their holiday, the furniture was unfrocked, and the house began to bustle with preparations for Grandfather McCall. Only young Harry knew his grandfather, and at such an early age this hardly counted.

The trip west followed immediately on the heels of Grandfather's successful campaign for the governorship. He arrived with his campaign manager, Charles Baxter, several days after we received the telegram. It was a happy reunion. Hal and his father talked long into the night. The following morning after breakfast, Mr. Baxter, in typical Boston city clothes, offered to go over to the hen house with me. Hal and his father were already out touring the ranch.

I had my doubts about Mr. Baxter's help, but I didn't want to hurt his feelings, so accepted his offer. He followed closely behind as we hustled across the ditch. As we neared the hen house, I turned to him and said, "When I get to that hen house, Mr. Baxter, I am going to catch a turkey and drag him back across the ditch by the legs. You just can't help me." Mr. Baxter made no comment as I hauled out the flapping turkey, and started across the ditch. Halfway across, he stopped me again. "Oh, isn't there something I can do, Mrs. McCall? I feel so useless."

"No, I don't think so, Mr. Baxter, because when I get over to the woodpile I'm going to pick up an axe and chop off this bird's head!"

Later when I was picking and dressing the turkey, Mr. Baxter inadvertently passed through the kitchen. Blood, feathers, and "insides" were spread all around the sink. His expression indicated that he must have thought that a young woman from Boston had come a long way from Beacon Street!

Grandfather McCall could stay only a few days. Because so many of our neighbors were anxious to meet him, we held an open house on the Sunday before he left and asked a few close friends to stay afterwards for dinner. After some of our guests left, Hal's father sat back in a big armchair before the fire and looked at his son, "Well, Hank, I can't tell you how impressed I am with the young men you had here this evening. Do you realize that way out here in this pioneer country, every fellow here tonight was a college graduate?"

We made our postponed trip east shortly after they left for San Francisco. Although the house was closed, Bill the caretaker was kept on through the winter to come in and check for frozen pipes. He discovered a leak in the third floor playroom and called the plumber. In fixing the leak, bricks were removed from the nursery fireplace and were left aside waiting for a mason to repair with cement.

Unfortunately, the caretaker was a little too anxious to have everything in order for our return, so when the mason didn't show up on schedule, he replaced the bricks without cement. The cook and maid, as well as Doug, were in the house when we came back exhausted late one evening. The lighted house and crackling fires were a welcome sight to tired travelers. Three drowsy children, after bowls of bread and milk, were put to bed in the nursery, where another fire blazed cheerily.

Soon afterward the grownups went off to bed. I had scarcely closed my eyes when I thought I smelled smoke. About the same instant I heard Doug shout "Fire!" as he jumped from his bed on the porch. Hal, pulling on a pair of pants and boots, rushed out into the cold night to the bunkhouse for help and to get the fire hose going. My brother and I rushed to the nursery to get Miss Haggart and the children to safety. Men hurried to attach the fire hose to the outside hydrant, which Hal had installed with this emergency in mind. The huge hose was dragged through the house to the second floor where the smoke was concentrated.

As Doug and I came stumbling down the stairs carrying the children, we were stopped in front of the guest room door by an amazing sight. Standing in front of a mirror was a young man fully clothed, carefully parting his hair! He had come into the ranch the night before.

"Don't you know the house is on fire?" I fairly screamed. As he turned to look at me, two men burst into the room dragging the fire hose, followed by Hal with an ax. While I stood by helplessly, with only time to tear a few pictures from the wall, Hal drew back his ax and smashed a portion of the north wall. It took several heavy strokes to lay open the pale yellow wall of my guest room and make an opening large enough to trace the fire. What we saw through the hole was a brilliant glow of a first-class fire snapping and crackling loudly. One of the main supports of the house was burned two thirds through before the fire was under control. If that beam had burned completely through, the entire house would have collapsed.

Calamities often come in threes. We had now weathered two devastating fires. Little did we dream there was to be a third one in the offing later that year. It took us months to recover from the shock of the house fire. We never left the ranch, even to drive into Redmond ten miles away, without stopping the car at the head of a grade a couple of miles from the ranch to look back. We fully expected to see a thin column of smoke bursting from the house. Sometimes we even drove back to be sure that everything was all right.

It was unusually cold the morning the big dairy barn burned. . . . Hal had become interested in dairy cattle although he was still running his beef herd—five hundred head of Shorthorns with registered bulls. Before this time, I believe, milking Shorthorns had been primarily used as dairy stock in Central Oregon. We had already had a start of registered Jerseys from Dreamwold; however, as the babies were weaned, Jersey milk proved too rich. It was then that Hal purchased his first registered Holstein, a big black and white animal—Lady Washington from Wisconsin. This was the start of the Holstein herd which ultimately became known all over the dairy world.

Both barns—a dairy barn and a smaller horse barn—were Dutch Colonial architecture designed by Hal. At the east end of the dairy barn was a machine shed connected to the small milk house containing all the farm equipment.

Below zero weather was routine in Central Oregon winters, but this year was colder than usual. The morning the barn caught fire, Hal had gone across the river to oversee the ice cutting. Our supply of ice for the year was cut from the river, hauled in, and packed in a sawdust-insulated ice house behind the main buildings. This provided the only refrigeration in those early days and the project was always an annual community affair. When the river was sufficiently frozen, the neighbors would get together and cut their year's supply of ice. It was a jolly occasion for the men, with a fire and a coffee pot waiting on the river bank. At intervals, the men would relax, swapping yarns and swigging the hot coffee.

As Hal left, he called to me, "Be sure to remind Willis about that blowtorch, Dote." With that, he went on across the river. When I finished the dishes, I started over to the barn with the message for Willis.

As I stepped out the back door and started for the barn, I saw Willis crouched down at the west end of the building. At the same time, a thin column of smoke shot up from the roof of the dairy barn, and I thought, *"Good heavens, Willis must be hurt and the barn on fire!"*

In the short time it took me to run over from the house to the barn, the entire roof was illuminated with a fiery gold. Suddenly I saw Willis coming toward me from the east end of the barn. Without a word, he threw me a rope yelling, "Take him out." I didn't realize until I was well outside that a large Holstein bull was on the other end of the rope!

In the meantime, men began appearing from all directions. From across the river, Hal had seen the blaze and started racing back, thinking the house was on fire.

In the machine shed was a brand new Studebaker car, as well as all the farm machinery. All hands started to push the Studebaker from the shed. But coming through the river the night before, the brakes had frozen. At that moment Hal appeared and jumped into the car and started the motor. Just as the car leaped forward, free of the shed, the entire barn roof and attached buildings collapsed in one explosive blaze.

I was well aware that a burning barn on the ranch stood little chance of being saved, and a barn with its loft bulging with hay is always a potential powder keg. It is not much more than a shell filled with combustible dried hay. A match, cigarette, or the blue flame of a blowtorch could touch off a holocaust. My message had not reached Willis in time. He had thawed a pipe at the east end of the barn, then gone on to thaw another pipe at the west end. The blue flame of the acetylene torch shooting invisibly into the brilliant sunshine caught a wisp of hay and soon the barn was in ashes.

Afterward, my husband patiently explained that the men should have saved the machinery first. But the ignorant young woman from Boston just couldn't bear to see the expensive new automobile going up in smoke—little realizing that the largest capital investment was tied up in the farm equipment.

Some winters, when our pipes froze, we would be without water for several weeks. Almost all the pipes ran on the north side of the house and froze easily. In the first winters, we were unable to cope with the frozen pipes, but after one or two had burst and flooded, we learned to shut off all the water and wait for a thaw. The kitchen was the most vulnerable. A flooding pipe would leave a thin coating of ice on the linoleum floor. Before we could crack it up with a hammer, the children would gleefully slide back and forth.

With the kitchen utilities cut off, I would move my cooking activities into the big laundry room on the far side of the kitchen. This room was equipped with an old-fashioned laundry stove of heavy black iron, with grooves at the side to heat the irons. It took a great deal of ingenuity to cook a meal, for only two pots at a time would fit on the top of the stove. It heated like magic but required a great supply of carefully split sticks of wood.

During these freezing periods, the early morning routine for the cook was vigorous. I would get out of my nightgown and into heavy riding trousers and overshoes. Then I would go downstairs and carefully pick my way across the frozen kitchen floor. Once in the laundry room, I would wait for my family helpers to bring in buckets of snow which we would melt. This was our water supply for cooking—and it takes a tremendous amount of fresh snow to make one pint of melted snow.

Once I had hot water, I could fix coffee and begin to cook a breakfast. Getting the breakfast together required real energy. For lack of space, I had to keep changing the cooking pots and pans from stove to floor.

After the first winter, with the enormous plumbing bill, Hal decided to do his own plumbing. He bought a complete plumbing kit. In later years, as his sons grew, he trained them to be plumbers too.

One night, with the temperatures way below zero, Hal was called out of bed by cattle drivers. They were moving cattle on down through the valley. When they saw our ranch lights, they had turned in, hoping for temporary food and shelter; they were nearly frozen. Hal asked me to get up and fix them some food. It just happened that I was prepared for any emergency. The day before, I had concocted a large kettle of beef stew; I also had a crock full of doughnuts in the cellar. It was a substantial meal I served those half-frozen men at nearly midnight.

Afterwards, Hal told the men they could sleep in the barn, and he gave them each a blanket. These blankets were unusually warm; they were from the Dreamwold racing stables—royal-blue imported wool with the Dreamwold crest. The men were gone in the morning and so were the blankets!

15. Red Cross Drive

Our trip back east in 1916 was the last we made before the
United States entered World War I in 1917. The allies were
suffering severe setbacks, the odds were against them, and an
intensive Red Cross Drive was under way in the United States
for money to buy food for starving Europeans. The drive
reached into every corner of the country, even the most isolated
spots, and I had been asked to canvass our area. So, one bright
morning I found myself soliciting for the Red Cross. The first
section allotted to me was sparsely settled Lone Pine Flat, up
over the rimrock; the second was a group of railroad camps.

Because I still felt somewhat like an alien, I was afraid my
money-raising trip would meet with little success. I felt that to
go knocking on doors of run-down farmhouses with my good
clothes and especially my Boston accent would simply antago-
nize my less fortunate neighbors. Even with my best efforts I
felt the Red Cross would suffer—and my premonitions proved
true. Few people were "at home."

After several fruitless stops, I came to a large, fairly prosperous-looking ranch house. The owner was a widowed, well-to-do
farmer recently married to a "mail-order" wife. After the marriage the farmer was seen less frequently in town and did not
mix much with his neighbors. His imported wife was scarcely
seen at all. She had a reputation as a mean, penny-pinching
shrew who had married the farmer only for his assets. When

repeated knocking brought no answer, I started banging. Presently I heard a faint rustling sound and the door opened a sliver's width. Then I saw her. She was recognizable from the vivid description—small, colorless eyes, a white face with a fierce look, and a small bony body.

"May I come in for a minute?" I asked, "It's about the Red Cross." The sliver narrowed. "I'll only be a few minutes. If you're busy, I'll wait. I'm in no hurry." So I sat down on the front step. After a short while the rustling noise was repeated and the door started to open. I jumped to my feet and grabbed the knob, at the same time shoving my foot in the doorway. I started my Red Cross "spiel." For most listeners I am sure it would have been stirring and touching, but now it was falling on deaf ears.

"It makes no difference how little you give, but we want to feel that everyone is behind this drive." She reluctantly opened the door wider but didn't ask me in. She then went over to the mantelpiece and took down a small leather purse. Opening it very deliberately, she counted out five copper pennies and dropped them into my hand. Then she gave me a shove and closed and locked the door without once having said a word.

When I told this story to a Prineville friend, who was spending countless hours soliciting for the drive, he told me of a heart-warming experience he had had when traveling the upper country above Prineville. "There was one little old place I deliberately passed up. I knew about them. They were both hard working, poor as paupers, with several kids. So I didn't want to embarrass them. But, believe it or not, coming back into town on that trip, I was flagged down by a woman at that farm gate. She was signalling me to stop. We exchanged greetings and she asked,

"You're travelin' for the Red Cross, ain't you? Well, here's our share." Then she handed me five one-dollar bills. "One of 'em's for me, one for the man and one apiece for the kids."

At this time the branch railroad from Redmond to Prineville was finally under construction and enough men were employed to fill three camps. This was my second section to canvass. The foreman of the company was a jolly little Irishman who met me and took me through the camps.

At the first excavation, it was hard to see through the brown dust. Huge, sweating horses labored up and down the banks, and equally sweating men shouted directions at each other. For a minute I thought I would give up and go home. Then from the opposite bank, through the haze, an evil-looking character with a black patch over one eye called out to me, "Say, Lady, if you're here for the Red Cross, stay away from me! Let Rockefeller do it!"

That settled it! I certainly would not give up. I said, "I wouldn't come near you with a cordon of police!"

When we finished tackling the rest of the men it was noon. The results were almost nil.

The foreman suggested we go back to the cookhouse, where dinner was under way. I told him about a previous talk I had had with the railroad contractor, who had promised that whatever sum I collected from the men, the company would double. The foreman agreed with me that that was a good idea. Also, with food in front of the men they would be in a jocular mood.

As we came into the cookhouse, he said, "Well, fellas, here she is and she's from the Red Cross. Better get ready to dish out your spare cash." With a friendly smile I started up and down the long table, tapping each man on the shoulder as I passed by. When we came away from the dinner camp, the Red Cross was $30 richer. As we came out of the cookhouse, the little Irish foreman said, "You don't know it, Mis' McCall, but all of us fellas thought your Red Cross Drive would be one big fat joke. We planned to let you try for a buck from the camps, but we felt damned sure you wouldn't get more than a buck. But when I saw you wallowing through the alkali dust up and down those excavations, I got an idea the joke might be on us—which it is—and now I'd like to add my buck to your thirty." With that, the little Irishman handed me a twenty-dollar gold piece.

16. The Prohibition Twins

Water was the pulse of the Central Oregon country and it sometimes ran rampant. In the 1918-19 winter, a heavier snow pack than usual in the Ochoco Mountains created flooding problems. Crooked River, swollen by spring thaws, was rising rapidly and seemed ready to overflow its banks. When Hal checked with the water master in Prineville, he was assured that the snow was now all out of the mountains. This meant that it would be unnecessary to jack the swinging bridge higher than its normal level.

Our beef cattle were pastured on grazing land above Bend and he made frequent trips there to check with his riders. Because we were expecting a new baby shortly, Hal usually left before daylight in order to be back by night. After he'd been to see the water master in Prineville, he planned to make an unusually early start the next morning. When he left with Bob, the Airdale, he was carrying a coonskin coat and a lighted lantern.

With the river rising rapidly I was extremely nervous. Because of the height of the river, our car was parked on the opposite bank. The river was roaring with an ominous sound.

Trying to forget my fears, I went back to bed and buried my head in pillows. I didn't want to watch Hal's lantern bobbing down through the field. All I hoped to see were his car lights coming on across the river, for then I would know he was safely on the other side. After a few minutes though, I couldn't resist the temptation to look out the windows. Then I heard a dreadful sound—a great wrenching noise of smashing lumber. There were no lights at all! I jumped from the bed. In a thin nightgown and barefoot, I ran down the stairs, through the hall, and across the lawn and fields toward the river. As I reached the main ditch and started down the bank, a figure loomed up in front of me. It was Hal McCall, dripping wet from head to foot. "The damned bridge went out!" was all he said.

Later that morning everyone on the ranch tramped down to the river to see what was left of the swinging bridge. It was lying twisted on our side of the bank with Hal's coonskin coat caught inside the coiled mesh like a fish in a net.

Warming up by the fire, he described what happened. As he reached the bridge with his lantern, the dog, Bob, trotted ahead of him. There was a small amount of water in the middle of the bridge. Bob went through and on across, but Hal, not thinking, jumped that little puddle. His weight brought the wooden planks down low enough in midstream to bring the terrific force of water against the bridge. It tore loose from the opposite bank. Hal turned to run back but quickly realized the fate in store for him unless he jumped clear of the bridge which was already beginning to buckle. As the bridge swung slightly beyond the swift, midstream current he leaped free and swam safely to shore.

By early June, it was time to make the trip to Dreamwold to fill the empty basket. I had been dreading this trip after reading about the crowded conditions and terrible food on the railroads after the War. We were taking all the children. Hal was going only as far as Chicago, where my sister, Marion, was to meet us and go on with us to Boston. I had been reading grim details of the high price and poor quality of food on Pullman trains crossing the continent. One cartoon in the *Saturday Evening Post* was of a fairly plump man boarding the Union Pacific in Chicago and being helped off in San Francisco practically a skeleton. For the week before we were to leave, I prepared food for our trip. I discovered an ideal container. It was a large, fiber-like suitcase which could be stretched to unbelievable proportions. In addition, I had a heavy Walker-Gordon zinc-lined box for liquids.* The day before we left, Hal walked into the kitchen and asked,

"What is that thing, Dote?" He was pointing at the container. I answered, "Just see, Hal, what's going in it." And I displayed the following: fried chicken, homemade bread, homemade cookies and doughnuts, a small Sterno lamp, a package of cream of wheat and jams and jellies.

There was little enthusiasm expressed by my husband and he said flatly, "I will not travel with that thing." I answered, "Then we simply can't go." Then I showed him my cartoon of the starved traveler. We took the food!

Traveling from the sagebrush in Central Oregon to Boston with a brood of small children was something of an undertaking. We had to leave the ranch at daybreak and drive to the little railroad station in Redmond ten miles away, where we boarded the train for the trip through the Deschutes Canyon. It took several hours to get to the small railroad flag-stop, Sherman, on the Columbia River. There we disembarked and stood beside the railroad tracks in the weeds and the dust and the sun until the big Union Pacific train came thundering in on its way to Chicago. Railroad officials never liked this stop, but our reservations had been made out of Portland.

As the Chicago-bound train came to a slithering stop beside us, the Pullman conductor stepped off looking disgusted. Suddenly the straw suitcase caught his eye. Pointing to our treasure chest he demanded, "Why don't you ship things like that?"

---

*In 1919, Walker-Gordon boxes (Chicago) were used extensively in many places for babies' milk. The box would hold eight baby bottles; iced, it would stay cold for considerable time.

As Hal herded the children onto the train, I turned to the porter. Holding out a crisp, new five-dollar bill, I said, "Will you please keep this Walker-Gordon box cool from here to Chicago?"

We had reserved a stateroom and, fortified with our goodies, hoped the trip would not be too unbearably hot. As it turned out, the weather was scorching and in that one Pullman car there were sixteen children—thirteen in the open car and our three in the stateroom. Marion met us at the station in Chicago. She had made reservations at the Blackstone Hotel, which had just been built. I had known many hotels in many parts of the world, but the Blackstone in 1919 was overwhelming. We certainly were a motley group in that elegant lobby—with our huge picnic hamper and Walker-Gordon box.

While my sister ordered supper sent up to our rooms, I peeled the clothes off three grubby children, pushed them all into the tub, and scrubbed them from head to toe. They fairly sparkled with clean faces and fresh pajamas when the taciturn waiter arrived. "Supper" consisted of a small platter of cold meats (sliced paper thin), a basket of rolls, and dishes of ice cream. While Marion signed for this sparse fare, the children yammered, "We want more, we're *hungry!*" "Quiet!" I admonished. "As soon as the waiter goes, we'll open up the picnic hamper."

Harry, who was then six and a half, folded his napkin with dignity and turning away from the table commented, "All I can say is, I *feel* just the same as when I sat down."

Such was the high cost of living in the year 1919 that the meager supper came to twelve dollars and fifty cents. The investment scarcely made a dent in those three small stomachs.

For several days Marion and I toured the children about Chicago, until a long-distance call came from our Dr. Washburn in Boston:

"If you want to have your baby on Marshall Field's counter, Dorothy, I'll come out and deliver it, but I think you'd be more comfortable having your baby at Dreamwold!" And it was at Dreamwold, on July 1, the hottest day of the summer, that the McCall twins came into the world. The date is well remembered by many, but for another reason: it was on this day that national prohibition went into effect. The twins, Samuel Walker McCall and sister Jean, have since been called "The Prohibition Twins."

17. Bootleg Island

Prohibition actually prohibited very little. It did, though, spawn a new and flourishing industry—the bootleg business. Strange mash produced lethal brews. With saloons closed, determined drinkers extracted alcohol from almost anything, even paint. Casualties were heavy, sometimes mortal, sometimes crippling.

In the Central Oregon country, many farmers—with long hours and small incomes for their strenuous work—turned to bootleg liquor for quick and easy money. One of our good neighbors, a father and grandfather, became a leading producer of really fine whiskey during those days. Many times I heard him say, "I have never sold liquor to a minor. If the law catches up with me and I am arrested, most of the leading businessmen in this part of the country will go to jail with me, for they are my clients. Without clients, I could not be in business." The law never caught up with him.

Stories about the Prohibition Era in Central Oregon would fill a lengthy book. One particularly good one concerned a man who had worked for us for many years. When he was finally able to rent a place for himself and his family, they settled on a nearby ranch, and eventually went into the illicit whiskey business.

When Federal agents came through the region to run down bootleggers, they usually tracked the operators "by their noses."

In other words, with nothing tangible in view, the smell of bootleg mash could be easily traced . . . and there was nothing tangible in view when our neighbor shoved his whiskey still on our side of the fence! Knowing our place as well as he did after all those years, it was easy for him to conceal the still. Its location was on a small island-like piece of land in a shallow part of the river where the green of the willows completely camouflaged "the plant."

When Federal agents, closing in, got a whiff from that willow-shrouded "island," the whole story came out. Just before the whole truth was established, however, our neighbor's son, Pete, was heard to say on the streets of Prineville, "What do you know . . . they found a still on old McCall's place!"

In the days before Prohibition, when late on some Saturday night we would be driving home from the movies in Bend—no lights would show up in the valley along Crooked River. But in those bootleg days, or rather bootleg nights, skies over the rimrock would suddenly light up around midnight. The great red flares were bootlegger signals. As the flares died down, the rumble of whiskey trucks coming out of the hills would shake the whole countryside. To us it was much more exciting than the melodrama we had just left in the movie theater in Bend.

There is another bootleg story which involved our big old Cadillac. Hal and I had driven down to Portland for a day or two in the summer of 1920. On the return trip, about sundown and without any warning, the old Cadillac just stopped. We were on a lonely highway twenty miles from Shaniko, a small pioneer town. There was nothing on either side of us but sage and juniper and there were no travelers on the road because it was the great American eating hour—the time of evening meal. Also, there was a good chance that traffic was over for the night.

Hal could find nothing wrong with the car, but we couldn't leave it there and trudge together to Shaniko. All our belongings were in that car, plus several crates of peaches for canning. And we couldn't split up, one staying and one going, for Heaven only knew what would have happened to a young woman in either case. As the sun went down, I thought it the loneliest place in the whole, wide world—not a sound except an occasional coyote call.

When we had almost made up our minds to sit it out for the night, around the corner came an empty bus. The young driver towed us all the way into Shaniko that night, against—as we learned later—the rules of the business and the garage owner. Towing stranded strangers in those parts was lucrative—at least in this instance.

Next morning, a large group of the town's citizens gathered in and around the garage where the Cadillac was grounded. I came in just in time to hear the mechanic's verdict, "It's the carbon point—worn out."

Behind me stood a tall, blond young man, very good-looking and wearing expensive, casual clothes (the heavy white silk shirt did not belong in Shaniko).

"Take the carbon point out of my Buick," he said. I looked at him in amazement and laughed, then said, "You must be a bootlegger!" Later, I heard much more about the good-looking man in the white silk shirt. He was known as "the king of the bootleggers" and ran a tremendous business up and down the coast from San Francisco to Seattle. One day, just as he was pulling away from the curb in San Francisco, a Federal agent jumped onto his running-board. Rather than risk killing the agent, he surrendered to arrest. The day he gave us the vital carbon point, he was, just like the Cadillac, grounded in Shaniko —with a fleet of high-powered, expensive cars impounded by the Federal Government. Even after paying tremendous fines and hibernating temporarily with the grounded fleet of cars in Shaniko, "the king" went back into operation and once more made his dangerous game pay splendid dividends.

Even the friendly, sociable town of Bend soon felt the insidious effects of Prohibition, and its local high school was not exempt.

Hal and I became frequent visitors in Bend shortly after we came back to the ranch from the Shaniko adventure. It was then that we met Ned and Ella Shevlin. Ned, a Yale graduate, was one of the partners of the Shevlin-Hixon mill.* Ella Shevlin had come originally from the South, but before joining her husband in Oregon, she had lived on Park Avenue in New York. We became great friends, and Hal and I enjoyed driving up to Bend for dinner and a game of *Chemin-de-fer*—a French card game. Sometimes we would go up early so that Hal and Ned could get in a game of golf.

Although times were beginning to be lean in the ranch country, Bend was booming. It was a beautiful little town with its surrounding snow-covered mountains, its Pilot Butte Inn, and quiet Mirror Pond formed by the Deschutes River. The Pilot Butte Inn, built by Philip Brooks, was an unusual building fashioned after a Swiss chalet and was certainly unique in Central Oregon. There were many fine residences, and a large hospital had been built in the downtown business district. Among the numerous other up-to-date buildings was the Capitol Theater. Soon Bend boasted the only golf course in Oregon "east of the Cascades."*

Among the little town's problems, though, bootleg liquor loomed large. Its availability to high school students was a real menace. My friend, Ella Shevlin, was horrified at the lack of enforcement of Prohibition laws. Together, we decided to do something about it.

We spent a great deal of time touring the country and talking to people. When word got around about us, we would often

---

*Ned was a nephew of Tom Shevlin, the famous Yale football player.

*My husband, a great golfer, once said, "Farmers and ranchers will never give up good farming land for a game. Bend will always be the one and only golf course around here." However, today, besides the very fine course in Bend, both Prineville and Redmond have excellent golf courses.

end up with a sizable audience and our efforts were fairly successful. When the law was finally repealed, Ella and I had a feeling of satisfaction. We had done our part!

But Prohibition was not the only exciting activity in the hills at that time. Later that same year of 1920, while I was in the East with the children, Hal wrote me an astounding letter:

"I've started to write you several times, Dote, about the great Silver Boom out here. I've held off each day thinking that tomorrow there would be even more exciting news to tell. My first letters were scarcely legible because I wanted you to know that, at long last, there is 'gold in them thar' hills.' It was not gold, but silver—trillions and trillions of dollars worth of it." Behind that letter was this story:

One day Roy Rannells, our foreman, came rushing up the back walk to meet Hal; almost breathless, he gasped:

"Hal, I think I've discovered the real bonanza—right here on the ranch!"

"Hold it, Roy," Hal said. "Calm down and tell me what you're talking about." Roy went on to explain that he had found a quartz vein carrying a high percentage of sulphide which looked like silver.

At the time, Dr. Herschel C. Parker, a noted professor of chemistry and physics at Columbia University, was staying with Hal at the ranch. Professor Parker was greatly interested in Roy's story. When he looked at the rock which Roy had brought over, he was even more impressed. The three men then held a conference and decided to investigate the discovery.

The next morning, Dr. Parker went into Redmond for chemical reagents for testing gold and silver. Among the reagents Dr. Parker had bought was sal soda borax and powdered charcoal. He bought only a few ounces of each, since there was no car available and he had to walk into Redmond, ten miles each way. From Portland, he ordered fire-assaying equipment—clay crucibles, scorifiers, and cupel cups. Next, the three men built a makeshift furnace in Roy's blacksmith shop over at the barn, where they could assay the quartz material.

The first test showed over two thousand ounces of silver per ton. Roy burst out with, "Wall Street never knew a mine like this!"

The first thing in the morning, Hal and the Professor were out of their beds and on their way to Redmond to buy all the reagents in stock at the drugstore, including most of a ten-pound bag of powdered willow charcoal. Both Dr. Parker and Hal very confidentially told the druggist about the discovery and warned him to keep it under his hat. As soon as Hal and Dr. Parker had left for the ranch, the druggist, unable to keep the secret, relayed the news to Dr. Hosch, the Mayor of Redmond. Within a few days the entire mountainside was staked in silver claims!

Every day, the three men assayed and repeatedly came up with a large quantity of silver about the size of a silver dollar. There was no change in the silver recovery, every button being about the same size. These results continued until the charcoal flux gave out.

During the evenings, the Professor and Hal would do a little assaying on their own. After supper, unable to relax, they would go upstairs to the guest bathroom to run a few more tests. At the time, this was the last word in bathrooms; equipped with many up-to-date nickel fittings, the large room was well lighted and heated.

Although the tests showed there was silver on Grey Butte, the big problem was how to dispose of the silver without flooding the market. Everyone with a claim was a potential millionaire. Then came the crash! The charcoal turned out to be silver antimony sulphide, and the sulphide in the quartz was iron sulphide.

Hal's letter went on to explain that "Some joker hoaxed us. So, Dote, the Grey Butte Silver Camp has passed away. All that is left is an empty charcoal bag and a number of people holding it."

When we came back from the East, I stepped into the guest bathroom and snapped on the light. What a shock! I had left gleaming nickel fixtures, but chemical fumes had transformed all these into dingy black. That dingy black is our only souvenir of the silver boom—and the fixtures remain so to this day.

18. The Grim Days

As the country edged into the disastrous depression days in 1929, and many people gradually pulled out of the area, Hal was concentrating on the improvement of dairy stock. He never "beefed" a bull. All that were raised were sold for breeding purposes. After eliminating the less hardy Dreamwold Jerseys, he started buying Holsteins in Wisconsin and Illinois. By 1921, he had established a dairy herd which became the foundation of Central Oregon's dairy industry.

At one time, the McCall Holsteins were known all over the world. A delegation of three men came all the way from Honolulu to the McCall ranch to buy Holsteins to start herds in the Hawaiian Islands. Others came to buy these registered purebreds from as far away as Japan and Peru.*

The county agricultural department was meanwhile encouraging enlargement of the dairy enterprise in Crook and Deschutes counties. They organized what was known as a "cow-testing association" and Hal McCall was a charter member of this group for many years. The McCall herd was enrolled for national testing as well, and this was adequate for all records, but Hal wanted to assist the county group—which probably could not have continued without his support.

Florence Idella Sharp was the McCalls' foundation cow. She was raised on the ranch and, at one time, was the second highest

---

*Redmond *Spokesman*, August 22, 1955.

producer of butterfat of any cow in the world. Florence set three consecutive records of more than a thousand pounds of butterfat in one year, and she would have ranked first if it had not been for a blunder. Our head dairyman, Stevens, was supposedly reliable, but when Hal was unexpectedly called away on a trip to Seattle, he proved far from reliable.

Milkings for the tests were important; they had to be done every six hours around the clock. Worried about the responsibility the day Hal left, I stayed up until after midnight, waiting to see the light come on in the bunkhouse. When no light appeared, I pulled on some clothes, grabbed a lantern, and marched over to the bunkhouse.

Pounding loudly on the door, I demanded, "Hey, Stevens, are you going to get out of bed and milk Florence tonight?" No answer. With that I thumped louder. Finally, a sleepy voice said, "Huh? What's the matter?" Again I demanded, "Are you going to get out of bed and milk Florence?" With no show of concern he replied, "I guess I got to get myself an alarm clock." I retorted, "Well, *I* guess you'll have to get yourself another job!"

For the following three nights of Hal's absence, the light in the bunkhouse came on at midnight. However, Stevens lost us the world's championship.

It was remarkable that Hal, who had had no previous experience with livestock, especially dairy cows, should make such a success of dairying. He had had some banking experience and had worked for one summer on the Grand Rapids (Michigan) *Herald* for Senator Arthur Vanderberg. But whatever Hal did, he did thoroughly. The slogan of his old school, St. Mark's, is *Age quod agis* (do what you do) and he had already lived up to this. People in the area were amazed at his knowledge of the intricate details of the registered dairy business. A man who particularly disliked Hal once commented after driving to town with him, "Think of that fellow having all them figures in his head. He quoted Holstein records all the way into town."

When beef went to ten cents on the dollar after World War I, Hal was unable to maintain his beef herd. And he was not alone —many cattlemen were forced out of business. Some met the problem by blowing their heads off.

Stockyards were grim in those days. Men walked the railroad ties through our ranch with packs on their backs, asking for work for three meals a day. No one had any available cash to spend but people on ranches always had plenty to eat. In contrast, throughout the large cities in the United States, breadlines were forming; and as conditions became more strained with unemployment, panic gripped the nation.

Our Holstein-Friesian Dairy was kept in operation because we still had a fairly good business with three large major consumers, including St. Charles Hospital and the Pilot Butte Inn in Bend. Our milk truck still headed for Bend—thirty miles away— before daylight. However, there was great loss in the door-to-door trade.

On the return trip from Bend, Hal always stopped at a grubby outpost close to the Redmond Railroad Station. Encampments of this kind for the down-and-out were called jungles, and that is exactly what they were—"Hobo Jungles." Homeless, wandering men riding the rails would get off at the Redmond Station or some other, and a group of them would pool their meager belongings—a broken coffee pot, old clothes, and any food they had. When Rancher McCall drove into the Redmond jungle with his milk truck, he was greeted with shouts of joy by the scarecrow derelicts. From his truck, Hal gave the men bottle after bottle of rich, fresh, sanitary milk, and to them he became a symbol of the good things of life that seemed to have passed them by.

Hal weathered a series of crises but there were severe setbacks. His beef-cattle herd—five hundred Shorthorns and registered bulls—carried a mortgage which was renewed every year. In addition to these beef problems, Hal inherited problems from both Father and my brother Douglas. Though Father had given us much, he had also left a great deal of unfinished business in Oregon. Hal eventually liquidated the pig investment, and he had put Doug's ranch up for sale. When my brother entered World War I, he planned to come back to his ranch and go on with his business there. As it turned out, though, my brother never came west again and Hal had to dispose of both his ranch and livestock.

The mortgage story really begins immediately after World War I. It had been the custom ever since he had the beef herd for Hal to go into Prineville each January to see the banker there, pay the interest on the mortgage, and have the mortgage renewed. We had always been able to meet the obligations until the end of World War I, when our good friend, Tom Baldwin, president of the Prineville Bank, dropped dead of a heart attack. Mr. Baldwin's death affected the mortgage, but it did more than that; it also meant the loss of a dear friend. When we moved onto the ranch, the Baldwins were our first friends in that country, and from then on, Christmas would never have been the same unless the Baldwins celebrated with us at the ranch.

In 1921, we had known that Mr. Baldwin was not well, for we had received a note from him just before Christmas saying he would not be able to join us for the celebration. It was a great disappointment to us all—we would miss him. Shortly afterward, while in Portland with one of his daughters, Tom Baldwin died suddenly early one morning at the Imperial Hotel.

Hal realized that there would be a different president of the bank when he went in to renew the mortgage in January, but he was dumfounded when the new president would not accept the former agreement and insisted that the mortgage should include the dairy herd. Reluctantly, Hal had to meet his demand.

A year later, that president also died of a heart attack and a young man whom we knew well took over the bank. Again we were startled when he gave us the ultimatum that we must pay the entire mortgage or he would foreclose on the dairy herd. Soon after that, on a trip to Portland, Hal lunched with a good friend, U. S. Congressman Pat McArthur, who was also head of a new dairy loan company. He arranged for the loan company to take over our mortgage. Things were looking up—then, suddenly, within a few weeks, stalwart Pat McArthur died from a mastoid operation. The largest stockholder in the company, W. M. Robinson, became the new head of the dairy loan company. From then on, our troubles began in earnest, for the new man turned out to be a scoundrel.

Hal did not suspect that Robinson was dishonest until one warm summer day when we were eating lunch on the back porch. A car drove up to the gate. Hal walked out and welcomed two men and brought them in for coffee. They turned out to be father and son: one an elderly man, the other a man in his mid-forties.

Coffee in hand, the younger man turned to my husband and said with some embarrassment, "I'm here on Mr. Robinson's orders, Mr. McCall. He thinks that we should do something about the dairy cows."

"What do you mean to do about them?" Hal answered.

With even more embarrassment came the reply, "He'd really like to have us take them back to Portland with us."

"You're joking!" Hal said. At that, the older man, also ill at ease, broke into the conversation:

"Do you know, Mrs. McCall, that I once sold a saddle horse to your father, T.W.L.? It was a beautiful chestnut five-gaited saddle horse with cream mane and tail."

I was very excited, "Oh, that was Enchanter. How well I remember him, and my father riding that beautiful horse. Did you also sell him the half sister, Enchantress, which he gave to my older brother Arnold?"

From then on, the conversation switched to horses. Before the two men left, they made a pleasant, friendly tour of the ranch, admiring our fine horses. When they left for Portland, with handshakes all around, we were still talking about horses . . . And they left for Portland without the dairy cows!

For several months after this, Robinson left us alone, and we hoped we would be able to finish with him by the end of the year. But we were wrong. One spring day the following year, Hal received a telephone call from Redmond. From the one end of the conversation I could hear, it was evident that Hal was astounded:

"Planning to come out today? Has he the drivers and trucks all ready?" Hal listened for a minute or two, then went on, "You mean none of them will go through with the deal? . . . Or will some?" Then Hal added, "You know, money talks . . . I certainly want to thank you for warning me in time. I'll move right in to forestall them."

Bursting with curiosity I asked, "Forestall what?"

"Robinson's on our necks again. One of his men, Dr. Brown, the Portland veterinarian, is in town with money to hire drivers. He wants trucks to come out here to load the cattle and take them back to Portland. I'm on my way to Prineville to see Billy King. You know, King's brother-in-law, Dr. Edwards, owns all the land back of us over the rimrock to the county road. I'm sure he'll padlock the gate. Then, if Billy will drive with me, we'll go to Portland this evening. While there, I am sure we can do something about the mortgage."

With those words Hal left for Prineville.

About the middle of the afternoon, I heard a car coming in; then a man called out:

"Mis' McCall! Mis' McCall!" At the door was our old foreman, Roy Rannells.

"I just came in the gate, Mis' McCall. I saw Hal in Prineville and he said that Harry and Tom with your herdsman, Garfield, were supposed to be patrolling the fence. No one was there.

Now I've got to get right back. Hal's waiting for me in Prineville to hear what's going on."

"All right, Roy. Go back into town and I'll get Bebs to run me in a horse. I'll get right over to the gate and stay there until the boys and Garfield show up."

Just as I was going out the door to meet Bebs, who was on her Shetland with a horse for me, the telephone rang. It was Hal. "Everything is arranged, Dote. Billy King and I are going to Portland right away. I won't be able to come home before we start . . . Here's Billy; he wants to speak to you."

Then Mr. King's voice, "Are you there, Mrs. McCall? Don't be afraid of anyone invading my property. The gate is wired. If anyone cuts the wire and tries to come in, call the Sheriff."

"What will I do if they come in?" I asked.

"Get over to the dairy barn. Stand in front of those big sliding doors."

"Suppose they shove me and come on in the barn?"

"Take your gun with you, Mrs. McCall, and if they push you and open those barn doors, shoot."

A wail from me, "But I can't shoot straight. I might kill somebody."

"That's their headache," was Billy King's answer.

I hung up and walked thoughtfully out to the gate where Bebs had Black Babe waiting. Together we raced over to the gate; there we ran right into Garfield and the boys.

"Where in heaven's name have you been? Didn't you know you left the gate unguarded?"

Mr. Garfield spoke up, "There wasn't a cloud in the sky or a truck on the road, Mis' McCall, so we decided to snap up to the store to get some pop."

It was getting on toward evening by then, so I said, "I'll stay over here till dark for I feel almost certain they will not try to load the cattle at night. This man, Brown, is having a hard time hiring drivers to come out here. They're all Hal's friends."

So the three of them went on home and I continued my vigil riding up and down along the fence. When it was dark, I went home for a late bit of supper. The evening ended uneventfully despite my fears and Miss Haggart's, and we sat for awhile and dozed before the fire. Gradually we realized that no one would come before morning to take away the herd. We went through our nightly routine and wearily climbed the stairs.

However, before going to bed, we went up to the third floor to look into the playroom closets. In those closets hung my ghosts—my evening dresses from 1911 and on. Here were dresses which I had worn at New York horse shows and at the opening of the short-lived Boston Opera. But most important to me were the gown and lovely velvet cloak which I had worn to the great World War I rally dinner at Symphony Hall in Boston.

At that time, the Allies were on the run, and throughout the United States, governors were calling on their people to support the Allies. Because my father-in-law, Samuel W. McCall, was then Governor of Massachusetts, I went to the dinner decked out in a king's ransom of jewels and velvets. Dinner was served as we sat at small tables in Symphony Hall. Toward the end, Governor McCall stepped through the parted curtains onto the stage and received a rousing welcome. When the applause subsided, he thanked the audience and introduced a young man recently home from Belgium—a young man who had done much for the refugees in Europe. As Mr. McCall stepped back, a tall young man, very embarrassed, stepped forward and spoke to us. That sincere speech was probably the dullest sincere speech I have ever heard. The young man's name was Herbert Hoover.

Now the dress worn that gala evening hung with many others in the quiet ranch house—but suddenly they had acquired a new usefulness. Opening the closet door, Miss Haggart and I rolled up the registration papers for the dairy herd and carefully hid them in the long trains of those dresses. Without these papers, the black and white dairy herd would be simply grade cows to anyone coming to seize them.

Strange as it may seem, Miss Haggart and I slept soundly until morning. Waking by six to fix the men's breakfasts, I was in the kitchen when the men came over from the bunkhouse. I knew two of them well, but the third had worked for us only a short time. When Hal left, he had cautioned me, saying, "Keep your eye on Jack. He may have been planted."

Just before the men arrived, we had decided to test them by outlining the situation. All three listened with interest and assured us they were on our side. As it turned out, they were. When they started into the laundry room, where a table was set for breakfast, I saw a car drive up to the back gate. Hurrying to the door, I thought, *"This is it!"* But I was mistaken.

A tough-looking young man strode up the walk and knocked loudly on the door. When I appeared in the doorway, he said gruffly, "You Mis' McCall?" I nodded and he went on, "I dunno' why I'm here, but I do know I'd go to Hell for Bill." ("Bill," of course, was our friend, Billy King. He had sent his tough sheepherder—now standing in front of me—to protect the ranch while he and Hal were in Portland.)

I welcomed him briefly and, turning to the other men, said, "When you fellows finish breakfast, you can all go down to the river and bring me back some fish. Then I'll cook them for your dinner." They went on in to breakfast, and I went on frying pancakes. I had left the door half open.

As I bent over the stove, I had a weird feeling that someone was watching me. Glancing toward the door, I looked directly into the face of a little man in a city suit and a derby hat. I dropped the pancakes and screamed. The scream brought my men to their feet ready for action, but I waved them back, spatula in hand. Little Doctor Brown—the veterinarian who had come to town with the bribe money—never knew how near he came to disaster.

"I'm looking for Mr. McCall," he said.

I said, "Mr. McCall is in Portland. Who are you?"

"So he's doublecrossed me!" Brown exclaimed angrily.

"He hasn't doublecrossed you, Dr. Brown. He drove down to Portland at midnight last night to straighten out this mortgage mess. It's a pity that you didn't know the people in Redmond are our friends. A telephone call last night from one of the drivers you were trying to bribe alerted Hal to the fact you were planning to steal our dairy cows."

Now I was the angry one and my voice rose. "You won't get them, Dr. Brown, or your outfit either, so get the hell out of my kitchen!" (By this time he had edged across the threshold.)

The little city man was visibly shaken. "To think a girl raised in Boston like you, Mrs. McCall, could talk like that!"

My voice rose even louder: "Don't give me any of that soft talk, Dr. Brown. Before something happens to you, get out of my kitchen!"

He retreated hastily, and I gave a sigh of relief, as Billy King's last words came back to me.

We had now weathered two crises with Robinson, but we still had our dairy herd intact. Later on when things had eased up a little, I went down to visit a friend in Portland. Unknown to Hal, I had worked out a little plan of my own. While in the city, I would put on my best clothes, including sable furs and a valuable diamond pin. Then I would go downtown to Robinson's office. I was very curious to meet this man because—before Hal realized he was embroiled with a swindler—he had many times given a glowing description of the little loan company man. "He's not a very large man, Dote; he's lithe, rather thin, and has a tanned face with gray-blue eyes. He is sly but charming."

So I went down to his dingy building. I must have looked completely out of place, for the secretary who showed me into

Robinson's office seemed a bit startled. I have never had a more genial welcome.

"It's certainly good of you, Mrs. McCall, to come all the way down to see me. I have always wanted to meet you, and explain about the dairy herd. You must think that I am some kind of monster. This is quite wrong. You would be surprised if you knew how many important people deal with me instead of dealing with their own bankers. Of course, it's mostly a question of credit and they come to me."

I listened, hypnotized, as the man went on, "I'm very fond of your husband. I wouldn't hurt you or your family for anything. The dairy herd thing was a matter of business, and in the long run I think both you and your husband will be glad to see the end of this western country. Go home to Boston!"

I couldn't believe that this was the sly scoundrel who had almost sent Hal to his grave. As I shook hands, all the while looking at those gray-blue eyes and that handsome mask, I prayed to God that he was speaking the truth, but in my heart I knew he was lying.

When I got back to the ranch, I told Hal about my visit. At first he was quite cross with me, "I know your intentions were good, Dote, and that you want to help, but for Heaven's sake, stay out of my business!"

To this I answered, "I don't really mean to interfere, Hal, but of course I want to help. Also, one of the principal reasons I went to see Robinson after hearing so much about him was that I was curious to see for myself."

All was quiet for the next few months. Then, one day in late fall, the stranger appeared. It had been a hard day; Hal was short handed and he was working over at the barn. After the children and Miss Haggart had supper, I sat at the kitchen table, waiting for Hal, too tired to eat. On the plate in front of me was a single lamb chop. I put both elbows on the table, picked up the chop, and started to chew on the bone. I glanced toward the kitchen door. Tired as I was, I was startled, for facing me was a blond young man in a black leather jacket. I motioned him in with the chop.

"Whoever you are, do sit down. Would you like some coffee?" He sat down and accepted the coffee, at the same time apologizing for his visit.

"My name is Sam Alexander. I am here from Robinson, Mrs. McCall. He has sent me to move the dairy cows."

As I looked across the table at that young man, I could hear my father saying, "I believe in threes"; his office was 33 State Street and his telephone number in Boston was 333. This was Robinson's third try for the dairy cows, and I felt in my bones that this man, Sam Alexander, meant to deliver the goods to his boss.

Just then the kitchen door opened and Hal walked in. A little embarrassed, Sam Alexander rose to his feet, and he and Hal shook hands. Over another cup of coffee, they talked for a few minutes; then Hal went back to the barn.

"Do you know what you're doing, Mr. Alexander?" With a puzzled smile, he answered cryptically, "I'm beginning to wonder."

Quietly we talked over the unpleasantness of his mission. He did not seem the kind of man to pressure a person or to enjoy carrying out drastic orders of an employer. He went on thoughtfully, "I began to wonder about my boss, Mrs. McCall, just now when I shook hands with your husband. The hand I shook was not the soft, well-cared-for hand of an effete Easterner. Your husband's hand was rough and strong, the hand of a man who has worked hard and long at manual labor. In sending me to take the Holsteins forcibly, Robinson told me that he was really doing those poor misguided dudes a kindness, that you were not farmers." He paused, then added, "Now, I'm beginning to wonder about my own cows and the piece of land he sold me!"

Sam Alexander did not move the dairy cows, and the land Robinson sold him turned out to be two feet under water. Sam himself was just another victim of this scheming man who was eventually convicted and given a long prison sentence in McNeil Island Penitentiary.

This painful and controversial business was ultimately resolved but the scars still remain.

19. How's That for a Dumpy Rat?

The effect of the long-drawn-out mortgage troubles lasted well after we had weathered the crises themselves. If I thought the children remained untouched by their elders' worries, all I had to do was glance out the kitchen window and see them playing the "Mortgage Game." Engrossed in playing "Ranch," they were periodically interrupted by seeing the "Sheriff" arrive. While one of the girls engaged him in conversation, sister or brother would circle the house, leap on a pony nearby, and race up the road to a large stump which they called "Grandaddy." Under the rules of the game, Grandaddy would give the rider "money" and he would dart back to pay off the Sheriff just in time to save the "ranchers" from foreclosure. How simple it would have been if this had been real!

Before the children started school, our visiting Bostonians were concerned about their schooling in "this God-forsaken country." Harry and Tom's first year of outside tutoring was done by Mrs. Travis, whose lawyer husband built her the lovely green cottage nestled in the junipers a mile or two up the rimrock.

Every morning, we would start the little boys out in clean jeans and shirts. Barefoot and riding bareback on Old Liz, a sorrel pony, they would lope away for the Travis house. Then, for three hours, with Hal away in the fields, I would try not to be nervous about this unusual way of sending children off to school. Shortly before noon, I would hear galloping hoofs, and Old Liz would come into view, loping on to the barn. Often there would be no children on her back, but I would decide there was nothing to worry about. Sure enough, presently in the distance, I would see the two little denim-clad figures trudge into view.

By the fall of the next year, though, Mrs. Travis had left her husband, and the two boys, along with their little sister Bebs, went on to school across the river. The school usually had an enrollment of around twelve students with one teacher. It was the proverbial little white schoolhouse—one large room for all eight grades, and heated in winter by a black cast-iron, pot-bellied wood stove. Winters were cruel, and in the frequent below-zero weather, I would pack substantial hot lunches for the children, which they ate gathered around the fat black stove.

That year each boy rode his own horse; and Bebs, her Shetland pony, Dick—a Christmas present to her from Santa Claus the year before. Bebs found Dick standing on the front porch that Christmas morning, with a large be-ribboned holly wreath around his neck, and it was love at first sight for both of them. Later on, the twins, Sam and Jean, joined their sister in the one-room school house, after Harry and Tom had gone on to Crook County High School in Prineville. By this time the boys had graduated to a Model T Ford for transportation.

The three younger ones all rode to school bareback—and during recesses there was great competition among them as they raced up and down the country road. At times they would ride without even a bridle or hackamore, just holding on to the ponies' manes. This marathon they called "riding naked."

The twins were seven years old when they began school, but the nightly reading aloud had given them a good start. In two months, though, they had moved to the second grade. With all the reading aloud and the isolation of the ranch, the children naturally picked up Hal's and my Boston accent. When school closed in the spring, the entire student body, including the teacher, seemed to be speaking with a clipped English accent.*

Outside of school hours, the children had many happy hours of recreation. Hal himself never lost his contact with baseball. Every Sunday during the season, he played second base for the Prineville team. Saturday nights, Miss Haggart and I busied ourselves packing the next day's picnic lunch in the big straw English tea basket—plenty of fried chicken, homemade bread and butter, homemade cookies, and large bottles of iced tea.

On Sunday morning, after the breakfast dishes were done, we all piled into the old Cadillac and were off to the ball game! It was always a struggle with the children to get started in time for Hal to have a little practice. Usually he would be forced to get into his baseball clothes behind a juniper bush somewhere along the highway.

How shocked I had been when I first came to Portland to see the Sunday afternoon crowds going to the ball game. The first Sunday I saw them, I asked Hal, "Where are all these people going?" And Hal, who had already spent two summers in the West, of course answered, "To the ball game."

"To the ball game!" I exclaimed. "What ball game? This is Sunday!" And here I was, years later, packing a basket and going every Sunday to the ball game. As a matter of fact, Hal, the second baseman, played ball with local Central Oregon teams until his oldest son, Harry, then in high school, joined him, playing first base on the Prineville team.

Each year after the baseball season was over, Hal insisted we must have some church observances, at home at least. So on Sunday mornings he would read aloud from the Bible and insist that we all listen. Having gone to chapel twice a day for eight

*The combination of the Central Oregon drawl mixed with the Boston accent developed a unique manner of speaking which is a trademark of the family today (1968). Governor Tom McCall's critics have occasionally unfairly remarked on "his phony English accent."

years at St. Mark's School, he had a slightly different outlook on religion than his ranch-raised children. Before he had us all assembled there would be a wail, "Oh, Dad, let's get out of this dark living room and go out into the sun." "Let's all bowl on lawn." Or, "Let's toss a few balls." But Hal was very stern and insisted that we have some regard for the Sabbath.

The first year on the ranch, we were very lucky in having a friend, the Bishop of Western Oregon, Robert Paddock of New York. He was truly a great man. In Oregon, he drove a car, but in earlier days he had had to travel the country on a horse, much like the old circuit riders. Whenever Bishop Paddock conducted a service in Prineville, Miss Haggart, Hal, and I were very sure to attend.

On Sunday evenings we would nearly always have a Community Sing, when some of the ranch hands joined us around the piano. It was a delightful time, with the piping voices of small children blending with Hal's baritone. "Onward Christian Soldiers" would be the closing hymn. The Community Sing continues as a part of our ranch life today, and there is still an unusual medley of voices—only now from three generations.

And there were other events. In the colder winters the sloughs froze over, and sometimes the river. We then organized hockey teams with the children. Hal had played hockey at St. Mark's and I had skated in Boston with internationally known skaters; and, before my marriage, I had skated in Paris at the Palais de Glace . . . But the sloughs of Central Oregon were quite a contrast from what we had known before.

We had two teams: Hal captained one, Harry the other, with the children divided between. I was the goalie on one, though not a very good one, and Tommy was on my team. At our first game, the opponents shot a goal right between my feet immediately after the game started. Tommy, a little slow himself on skates, stopped short and demanded, "What's the matter with you?" I promised that it wouldn't happen again and told him to calm down. Really concentrating, I grabbed my hockey stick firmly when "whoosh!" the puck again went right between my skates. For a second I didn't dare look at Tommy—a plump little eight-year-old boy with a round face. But when I did look, I thought he was about to blow up and burst. His face at that moment was like a red balloon. With his blue eyes fairly popping, he hurled his stick across the ice and, pointing his finger at me—a bum goalie but still his mother—screamed, "How's that for a dumpy rat?"

20. "The World"

Toward spring, when the river was up, we were cut off from the county river road and school, and our only access to town was up over the rugged rimrock. Since we made these trips as seldom as possible, we had to create our own indoor amusements. The results included our own home orchestra, printing a newspaper, "The World," and our own puppet show. And, no matter what was going on at the ranch, summer or winter, good weather or bad, we always depended on our library. This, Father had given us when we left Boston. Though many were lost in the freight fire at Redmond, we still had many fine books, both adult and juvenile. Among them was a complete set of Everyman's Library, which comprised almost a thousand volumes. In giving us the library, Father had wisely predicted, "Out in that country, you will probably have to create your own school at times."

Light for reading was another matter. Because of the elements, we were often without electricity, and would resort to candles and lamps. Having had bitter experiences with fire, I kept the kerosene lamp in a fixture in the kitchen. When the electricity was off, candles were carried through the house in safe holders.

Besides the kerosene lamp in the kitchen, the only other lamp in the house was on the large oak table in the living room. This was a fixture — probably unknown today — called the Aladdin

Lamp.* It was a tall lamp with a spreading shade, and big and bright enough for the entire family to read by. Most of this reading was done aloud, especially in the winter evenings. At first, I was usually the reader; but gradually, starting out with the family, the evening reading group expanded to include many of the ranch folk. It took a little maneuvering to choose a book suitable for such a gathering, and Zane Grey often solved the problem. Hal and I eventually became librarians for many of the settlers on our side of the river.

"Pick me out a book, Mis' McCall," became a slogan as the years went on.

While we grownups were struggling with problems of isolation, wind, snow drifts, and swinging bridges, the children suddenly began observing these things through young reporters' eyes. They had established their own newspaper, *The World*, during the winter of 1926-27 when the river was flooded for three months and there was no school. Whatever was part of their life became part of that paper. In its lively columns, hens were murdered; rabbits born; pigs sold; and dogs fought and ticks bit children. People visited and the family went to town. All these events were reported, sometimes with exaggeration, usually with humor.

Tom, Bebs, and Harry produced *The World*—they wrote, illustrated, and circulated it. The first editions were in longhand, but eventually it graduated into typewritten and mimeographed form. The young reporters and editors tramped the hills and rimrock on our side of the river. They gleaned unbelievable news items from the homesteaders and from their own immediate family—as well as from domestic animals, coyotes, and rattlesnakes.

The newspaper was melodramatic and unique in its style of presentation and expression. At times it was even libelous. The

---

*A type of kerosene mantel lamp.

following excerpts illustrate the colorful imagination of the editors:

Big Dog Fight Stopped

Wooly and Tip, dogs of this city, were parted from a death grip by the bravery of Mrs. McCall of First Street. She rushed in and pulled them apart with her bare hands and chased the offending Tip around the house. She reports that he haunts her. She will be awarded a medal in the Town Hall next week.

The "city," of course, was the ranch; "First Street," the lane on which our house stands. Early in 1927, this story appeared:

Thief Escapes

Last night a man broke into the Ford shop of this city and took a car. The identity of the fellow was not known until today when it was learn that his real name was Calvin Ballord, alias A. Mallord, alias Sam Smith, alias "the fish."

Also in the same issue:

Pigs to be Sold

Mr. Tom McCall, it has been reported, is planning to sell his pigs. They will average 200 lbs. and will make a fine dinner for someone.

Large headlines introduced this exciting lead article:

Tick is Discovered!

Tom McCall of this city discovered a giant tick on his chest. He quickly called 8 doctors whose combined efforts finally dislodged the insect.

(He should of used "Innes Insecticide" for hens and humans—*Paid Advertisement*)

Included in the regular format of this Hearst-type of report-ing were short stories by author Bebs McCall, weather reports, and "Health Letters and Questions" by Tom McCall, under the pen name of Andy Hump. In this column, the "tall silk hat" re-enters the news. Years after Hal McCall stood on Western-wold's porch after the fire, wearing his khaki pants and tall silk hat, his young son Tom wrote,

> Dear Doc: Every time I get a cold draft my hat catches pneuma. It is a tall silk one and what do you think I can do about it? Please answer quickly.
> Yours Sincly.

> **Answer:** This disease of the hat cannot be cured. The only thing to do is to get a cap that hangs low about the ear to protect it from the cold.

Other Health Talks discussed the throat and wrists:

> The throat should not be rasped by un-healing tobacco or alcohol, says Mr. Hump. Neither should you swallow bolts.

> The wrists should be large, bony, red, hairless and serviceable. One should never slash them with an electric saw as this sometimes proves serious. Also, never bind them tightly with barbed wire as some-times the barbs enter the wrist and may prove painful. Whenever your wrists get hairy, Mr. Hump advises you to use Hatches Hair Healer.

Stories of Crooked River and its importance to the ranch appear in nearly every issue, although in the editor's own inimitable fashion:

River Rising

Crooked River is rising rapidly because of the warmer weather. Many bodies are said to be floating down from the upper country.

Almost a month later the river apparently was still rising:

River is Rising

The river of this city commonly known as Crooked is rising rapidly. Many refugees have come floating down on rafts and have been taken in by the kindly but simple, Mrs. Henry McCall. There are now about 35 here and have been entertained by Miss Bebs McCall at cards.

Dog Plays with Death

Tip, dog of this city, played with death today when he plunged into a roaring torrent (Crooked River) after bits of wood thrown therein by his children friends, Bebs and Harry McCall of 1st St.

Readers of *The World* who were unfamiliar with life on the ranch might have been puzzled by frequent references to the "urn." A March 13, 1927, issue offered this news item:

Mr. and Mrs. Henry McCall of this city will start early tomorrow for Portland. As there is a conspicuous absence of a certain commodity around these parts, they plan to bum a ride down and when there, rob a bank. In the murky morning stillness they will undertake to run the gauntlet of hungry creditors in the famous urn belonging to G. Osborn. Any contributions to this trip will be gladly accepted by the surrounded travelers.

The "urn" mentioned was a car belonging to our hired man, Glen Osborn. Its name stemmed from the fact it was bowl-shaped and topless. When the editors rode in the "urn," they felt as though they were riding in a bathtub.

Glen and another hired man named McJunkin figured prominently in *The World*. McJunkin emerged sometimes as a hero, in other issues as a "heavy."

Man is Vicious

When he saw his innocent children sleeping sweetly, Henry McCall of this city, cursing and foaming at the mouth, hailed them out of bed with a cudgel. The screaming children ran down First St. and into the arms of C. McJunkin a hired man. Mac soothed them and then beat up old McCall. If it happens again McJunkin says he will report it to the S.P.C.C.

Man Starts Feud

A feud has started between "Doc" Clark and C. McJunkin his uncle. It is a real old mountaineer one and is expected to last at least three generations. Mac is not well-liked in this community so our sympathies are with the Clark faction.

McJunkin appeared in one edition as a man suffering from a broken heart. Further down the page he was reported as being completely cured by "Dr. Blossoms Remedy for Colds and Cattarh." When Glen Osborn procured wood, the incident turned into a full-fledged Indian War:

Wood is Gotten!

Some wood was gotten today by G. Osborn, speed record breaker, and was delivered at the residence of H. McCall after much trouble. He was attacked by several bands of Indians and held up by bandits all after the precious luxury. He bravely slew 57½ Indians with a pitchfork and thundered into town covered with blood and nearly exhausted.

The World was not above making retractions:

Mistake Made

A hideous mistake was made by a common local paper when, from reports, a news item was as follows: "LoVelle Lott of Terrebonne spent the weekend with 'Bob' McCall of Crooked River." Miss Bebs McCall is very insulted by being called 'Bob' as she has been in this country for years.

Headlines such as "Birds Heard," "Bantams Freed," and "Hold Your Beef, Prices Rising" attest to the children's awareness of ranch life. One story was written up under:

Drakes Enraged!

Sir Sidney Rodney, drake of this city, was found pursuing a young blade of a rooster down Third Street. In the course of his rage Rodney tore down several buildings and injured one chicken. He was not responsible as the rooster had been insulting Lady Rodney.

Throughout the life of the paper, Hal McCall emerges as a principal source of news and a focal point in the children's lives:

Man Takes Secret Trip

Mr. Henry McCall of First St. left the city limits this afternoon. When asked where he was going he winked and took off his hat. He expressed a wish to take a gun but was frustrated by his worried wife. He is said to have periodical fits of wanderlust.

Hens are Murdered!

Two hens, known in this city, were found brutally murdered on an old wood pile near the Doctor Clark place. Henry

McCall, who was caught nearby, was grilled and confessed but it is suspected that he is only a tool of some power.

Man Wins

Henry McCall of First St. beat his son Harry 2 games of checkers. Harry is whispered to have given it to the old man because he had been working all day. Harry sometimes showed his stuff but when Henry pouted, he stopped.

At times, an editorial note crept into the news:

Editors go on Trip

The editors are planning another trip, for the purpose of getting the mail. They also plan to observe the natural and artificial wonders of this planet. If more people did this, the world would be better.

The World nearly ended publication before it started. In the first issue this item appeared:

Editor's Staff in Danger

The editor's staff of The World was in danger of complete annihilation when Bebs McCall spilled a drop of red ink. Mrs. McCall of First St. discovered it and for a time it looked pretty dark for the editors but it all ended well.

Mrs. McCall of First St. came into the news again:

News
Woman Pestered

Mrs. Henry McCall of First St. was "pestered" by The World's reporters for news. After several hours of such pestering Mrs. McCall threw a large spoon at the offending reporter.

Man Perfidious Says Woman
Mrs. Henry McCall of this city says
that Collins Elkins her grocer was a "Perfidious wretch" because he sold her some
poor spinach. Just yesterday Mrs. McCall
announced she "did like Mr. Elkins." We
think that Mrs. McCall is the perfidious
one.

Their weather reports were much more colorful than the
present day "ninety per cent chance of rain"; A. Smith, *The
World's* meteorologist—whose futuristic telephone number was
101-11211111—included helpful suggestions with his reports such
as, "Big Storm Coming, Close Your Windows."

The World continued regular publication through the winter
and into the spring of 1927. The children's Aunt Marion in Boston had spent some of those "isolation" months with us on the
ranch and had been kept informed of ranch events by the enter-
prising journal after her return east. Her appreciation prompted
the following telegram to the newspaper editors: "Am sending
you a fifty-dollar check to underwrite past enjoyment and continued publication and prosperity." Upon receipt of the telegram and the "incentive" money, the editors staged a joyous
celebration and promptly ceased publication of *The World*.

21. Music in the Sagebrush

While the older children were publishing their newspaper, the twins embarked on a money-making project of their own—the commercial raising of rabbits. The idea originated after seeing their older brothers trapping and selling muskrat and beaver hides they had obtained from Crooked River. It was just another outgrowth of the forced self-sufficiency on our ranch.

Sam and Jean used one of the unoccupied buildings near the barn for their rabbit projects. The commercial end of this business, of course, was left to one of the men on the ranch who was well versed in slaughtering and dressing animals for market; but Sam and Jean had the fun and interest of rabbit-raising. The twins would always bid good-by of an evening to their pets as slaughtering time approached.

Also during this period, Harry became the owner and producer of a puppet show, which became a popular entertainment. After Christmas, he came down with virus pneumonia. This proved serious enough to keep him out of school the rest of his junior year. However, his creative brain got to work as soon as he was out of bed and able to get around the house.

He started to make a puppet with materials at hand: tin cans, three or four drawers of cloth scraps, needles, and spools of thread. We all marveled at the unsuspected adeptness of his baseball-playing fingers. That first puppet eventually became many, and Harry staged his first production, "The Wizard of Oz."

To the most minute detail he created a tin woodman (from the cans), a straw man, and Glynda the Good—along with several other minor characters.

We were all invited to attend the opening night performance. The dining room drapes were drawn, and the family and neighboring children were seated in the hall. Bebs opened with a piano solo, the curtains parted, and the show was on! . . . "The Wizard" was followed by other fairytale plays until their creator was able to be outdoors again.

We now had three older children in high school, and with money becoming scarce in the ranch country, we were often hard put to buy necessary clothing and supplies for them. Once more, Father came to the rescue. Through the years he had given us some wonderful guns, and our arsenal at the ranch compared with the best in the country. On one occasion, Father had The Colt Company, and Smith and Wesson competing to turn out the most beautiful pair of revolvers for his daughters. One pair, in a black leather case lined with blue velvet and created by Colt, was silver and mother-of-pearl. The etching on the silver was exquisite. This set was for my sister, Bunny. Mine was the set by Smith and Wesson—in a similar black leather case but lined with red velvet. The guns were gold and mother-of-pearl.

I now call the gold guns my "educational guns." At the start of the school year, I fell back on my gold guns for a few hard-to-come-by items necessary for high school children. The squeeze was on until harvest money came in.

Every fall in the bad years, I put on my best clothes, took the guns, and drove to Bend to the Palace Pool Hall and Mr. Harold Klein—the owner and a fine man. On the counter I laid the beautiful pair of Smith and Wesson revolvers. In turn, Mr. Klein handed me $100; then into his pool-hall safe went the pistols. After that we shook hands and I drove away. Late in the fall, the trip to Bend would be repeated, only this time into Mr. Klein's hands went my $100 and out of the safe came the guns. In all the years that the "educational guns" were in transit, Harold Klein never charged a penny of interest.

On one of these trips, as I took the guns out of the case, I became aware that someone was watching me closely. I turned from Mr. Klein and was face to face with one of the most evil looking characters I had ever seen. Turning back to Mr. Klein, I whispered, "Won't men like that break open the safe some night and take my gold guns?"

Harold Klein burst into a hearty laugh as he patted me on the shoulders and said, "Well, Mis' McCall, that's your headache."

The late 1920s took their toll not only economically but also personally. As the years went on, we were left more and more with a feeling of aloneness. There were no longer the pleasant, happy visits with our family and friends from the East. One by one they were slipping away. Too often, we would receive the word of their passing. News of Father's death in 1925, after a long illness, saddened us. Everywhere we looked on the ranch, there were reminders of him.

But children can be relied on to chase away gloom and discouragement, and our five were no exception. One year the older children formed an orchestra, which had its beginnings at a Christmas party. That year the boys found under the Christmas tree a toy-sized ukulele, a banjo-uke, and a small drum—all merchandise from Santa's agent, Montgomery Ward.

Tom took to his ukulele right away, Harry performed very well with the banjo-uke, and one of their friends was able to get a fair amount of rhythm out of the small drum. Bebs, however, was the only trained musician. She had been taking piano lessons for several years from Dr. Charles Edwards' wife in Prineville. The family had originally come from San Francisco, where Mrs. Edwards was well known as the granddaughter of James

King of William.* Her career as a brilliant pianist had been cut short because of an accident to one of her fingers. After marriage to Dr. Edwards, she moved with him to Central Oregon, where she taught music.

Since Bebs played the piano well and could transpose the music, she made the arrangements. Almost overnight, we had a small, dedicated group of musicians in our midst. Their eagerness to practice and expand their experience was limitless. One morning as I was leaving for Portland, the children rushed out to the gate carrying a large jelly jar full of coins—nickels, dimes, and quarters.

"Will you please take this money, Mother, and try to find us a set of trap drums?" they clamored.

Dumfounded, I answered, "For heaven's sake, then get some sort of sack for that money. I can't carry it all in a jelly jar!"

That day on the crowded bus, I got into conversation with an attractive young woman sitting next to me. She was on vacation from Sherman-Clay—the largest music store in Portland at that time—and she told me of the company's sincere interest in junior orchestras; also of the encouragement they tried to give to aspiring young music-makers. By the time we reached Portland, the young woman had learned all the details of our Montgomery-Ward orchestra.

The following day, on my friend's advice, I made a trip to Sherman-Clay and talked to a young man in charge of junior orchestras. He was greatly interested in the venture, and most cooperative. We settled on a trap-drum set for $32.50. I emptied my money-sack of nickels, dimes, and quarters, which amounted to $7.50. To this I added $2.50 to complete a $10 down payment, the balance to be paid in two installments.

When the drums arrived at the ranch, there was great excitement and the children started to practice immediately. Hal and

---

*James King of William was the crusading editor of the *San Francisco Bulletin*. His murder, at 27, resulted in the forming of the Vigilante movement, that eventually cleaned up crime in San Francisco.

I put up with the racket and loss of sleep for some time; we realized the importance of practice. And every day the instruments began to sound better and better. It was not long until the orchestra was being signed up for Grange dances under the impressive name of the Dirk Vodka Orchestra.

One hot afternoon when practice was in full swing around the piano, several women came picking their way over the back ditch from the road which led to the house. (Irrigation was in progress and no cars could get through the water for twenty-four hours.) I left the living room and hurried out to the gate to meet them. They turned out to be friends from Portland, supporters of the symphony orchestra there. The windows and doors were all open and music was pouring out as I greeted them.

"For goodness' sake, Dorothy, *what* is going on here?"

"Oh, it's the children's orchestra," I explained.

"However did it come about, 'way out here in the sagebrush? It is really good." My answer seemed to surprise them:

"Oh, it all started with that great mail-order house, Montgomery-Ward!"

As practice brought results, the original Christmas instruments were discarded for better ones: Tom's for a good saxophone, Harry's for a fine banjo. The trap-drums were now paid for in full, and the popularity of the early Dirk Vodka Orchestra had spread throughout Central Oregon. The group was in demand, with engagements almost every week-end. During bad weather—when all practices were forced indoors—the elders had their problems: some nights the orchestra worked into the wee hours. One bright morning, I stepped onto the sleeping porch to find all three beds neatly turned down just as they had been left the night before. Before I could call for Hal, the telephone rang.

"Mrs. McCall?" . . . it was the operator's voice . . . "We've been trying to get you since five o'clock this morning. Your orchestra got stuck on Comb's Flat in that 'dobe mud, coming

153

down to Prineville from the dance. Two had to leave the car and walk to town for help. Don't you and Mr. McCall worry . . . they're all okay!"

"Worry!" I must have shed ten pounds when I saw those empty beds!

One memorable trip we made with the orchestra was to the little town of Mitchell several miles above Prineville. We had had a lot of snow that winter and Hal knew the roads would be bad over the Ochoco Mountains. But this trip was a high spot with the orchestra because the four players would receive fifty dollars for their performance. Hal had agreed to transport the orchestra to Mitchell in the aging Cadillac. Because he knew it would be slow going and a long, hard trip, we made an early start in the afternoon. We were all well bundled in winter togs.

Hal piloted the car through huge snowdrifts and down into the little town, now crowded with fun-lovers from miles around. It was Washington's Birthday, and this February dance had become a traditional event in Mitchell, with couples coming from as far as fifty to a hundred miles away.

As we came into the small hotel, I called up to a group of friends, who were standing on the second-floor balcony, "Have any of you a room up there where Bebs can change?" Before the dance, Bebs, the piano player, had to slip out of her slacks and into a black velvet dress. A handsome young man I recognized from Prineville, on the upstairs balcony, stepped forward with uncertain balance and, looking down at me with glassy eyes, motioned Bebs and me up the stairs, saying, "Oh, yes, you can have our room, come right this way, Mrs. Whiskey!" The party was certainly off to a good start!

That was a night the orchestra would long remember; they played until four o'clock in the morning and Bebs, the twelve-year-old pianist, nearly dislocated a finger pumping the old piano keys. Dawn saw us all again bundled into the Cadillac and on our way home. As we came down the mountain slopes, sunlight peeked through the snow-covered evergreens. The orchestra members were still exuberant, though beginning to get sleepy.

"Gee, Dad, just think—fifty dollars for one night!" the boys chuckled delightedly.

Yawning and hanging onto the steering wheel, Hal's answer was, "They'll pay me fifty dollars flat before I make a trip like this again!"

22. Dude Ranch

In the summer of 1930, after the crash of '29 and the resulting Great Depression, our friend Becky Wood stopped for a short visit on her way to the Ochoco Mountains from Portland. Every year Becky made the trip up to the country above Prineville. She was a great lover of wild flowers and had told us many times that there were more varieties of wild flowers in the Ochoco Forest than in any other place in the world. Furthermore, Becky had traveled extensively enough to be an authority. On this trip her teen-age daughter came with her.

As we stepped out onto the balcony into the warm sun that day, Becky turned to me and asked, "Would you let me leave Becks (her daughter) here for a month? She has had a double-mastoid operation. If she could sun-bathe here on this balcony every day, I know it would do her a world of good—and she would be a paying guest."

She went on, "Wouldn't a few young paying guests be a good idea for you anyway, Dorothy?" I was surprised.

"I really hadn't ever thought of such an idea."

"Why not, Dorothy? You and Hal have five children in this big house, and they apparently have everything to entertain young people—ponies, saddle horses, a tennis court, and acres of land to explore. They are expert riders and could teach non-riders. Then, there are the rimrocks and the Butte to climb, the river to swim in, and your wonderful library. Not to mention that giant playroom on the top floor! That room alone could furnish entertainment for all ages."

During the years when the young McCalls had occupied the nursery-playroom, it was carpeted from wall to wall with a comfortable pale gray carpeting. On this, Harry McCall, the mechanic, set up his first electric railway. Through the years railway cars of all descriptions rolled in and out of stations, through a life-like miniature scene. Birthdays and Christmases always saw additions to the rolling stock.

The far corner of this large room was called the "Dolls' Apartment." Small furniture of all kinds and occupants of all descriptions and nationalities, black as well as white, still occupy the "Dolls' Apartment." It is watched over by Alice of Wonderland, a most life-like, almost human, little girl. Alice was sent from Paris during World War I by my sister, Marion, then a war nurse. This lovely figure is flexible. Her facial coloring is realistic and her eyes look at you from a head set on a swan-like neck. Nurse Jemima sits beside her watching over the Raggedy Annes and Andys, the Goldilocks, the little stuffed dogs, and cats. No one ever disturbs the Dolls' Apartment, for three generations have believed, as do any readers of Raggedy Anne stories, that at night the nursery comes alive and all these little people have happy, gala times.

Here in the playroom is the carriage with a black and white horse in which I used to wheel little Tommy McCall around the ranch, with Harry trotting beside him. The little white rocking horse lives here, and last but not least, looming up over all when a visitor reaches the top steps and catches a first glimpse of the nursery-playroom, is Pegasus; the great white rocking horse in his gold and red velvet trappings, on his head a proud red and white plume. Horsemen in Central Oregon have many times checked Peg's hide to find that he is made from a real pony's skin. His brilliant painted stand is screwed onto an enormous rocker. Little children are fearful when taking even an easy ride; Peg is so high.

As I listened to Becky, I found myself becoming enthusiastic about having other young people at the ranch. Both outdoors and in, daytime and evening, the great house would be perfect for both small children and teen-agers. Even during a depression, rich people would still spend money on their children.

Becky continued, "Why don't you take in several young people on the same basis as Becks? If you and Hal agree, I promise you I can fill your ranch to overflowing." She laughed and added, "You'll have the first Junior Dude Ranch in the country!"

Hal was at first reluctant when Becky broached the subject to him, but she finally persuaded him that the children would have great fun and the association would be a healthy experience for all. The three of us finally decided that a reasonable charge would be $35 a week or $140 a month; that we would accept children from eight to fourteen years of age, and would start with four or six. It would be best to divide the "guests" into two groups: the older ones would be with the teenagers, Harry, Tom, and Bebs; the younger ones would be with the twins, Sam and Jean, then age eight. This plan would provide varied entertainment for the different age groups.

Becky Wood was as good as her word; shortly thereafter we were fairly swamped with telephone calls. Because Hal was busy operating the ranch, Miss Haggart and I looked after the incoming guests; at least so they thought. But after the first two weeks, our fine cook was called home by sickness in her family, and the cooking fell to Miss Haggart and me. As it turned out, we went through the entire season with cooking included in an already-busy summer schedule.

Right away we developed a regular daily routine. Early in the morning before their own breakfast, the children went out to feed and water their horses. This was a must! It took an initial week of constant reminding, but after that there was no problem. When breakfast was over, all were turned loose for outdoor activities. These were varied and included riding, hiking around the ranch, tennis, and baseball. The towering rimrock behind the ranch, as well as the picturesque butte to the west, lured all ages. Before a climb, Hal—who was usually in charge—always briefed them on rattlesnakes, how to recognize them, and what to do if they met one. As a rule, though, we had learned that rattlesnakes were slow to strike unless annoyed. On days when hikes did not interfere, dinner—the main meal—was served between noon and one o'clcok. It was the biggest meal of the day and was followed by the siesta hour for the very young. All the older children were interested in my explanation of the siesta hour in Rome! There, in the heat of the day, all activity in the city ceased abruptly; even the stores closed.

One story about the siesta—involving my strong-minded sister, Marion—particularly intrigued them. The occasion was when we were living with Mrs. Maude Howe Elliott* in her apartment in Italy. Marion thought the whole idea of a siesta was foolish, so she pranced out into the hot sun in her own independent way, despite admonitions. It was not long before she came back and promptly fainted.

"So," I would say, turning to the younger children, "You must now take a nap in the middle of the day." To the older ones I would say, "Do whatever you please for two hours. Read or play checkers or just play, but stay in the house! At four o'clock we'll go swimming."

Soon after four, we would gather on the front porch and start out the gate for the river. We made a colorful procession stalking through the grain fields in our bathing clothes and flat coolie hats.

The deep swimming hole and the shallow beach on the other side of the river were ideal. The little children would trot across

---

*Mrs. Elliott, the former Maude Howe, was the daughter of Julia Ward Howe, author of the "Battle Hymn of the Republic."

the foot bridge and frolic with their water-wings on the opposite side of the river. Meanwhile, from the high banks on our side of the river, the older children dived from the high bank and swam up and down. The rays of sunlight filtering through the leaves of the willows caught the ripple of the water and sparkled on the reflections of the lively children . . . Without the relaxation of the swimming interlude, it would have been difficult to carry on my duties for the remainder of the day.

Becks Wood wrote regularly to her parents about the wonderful time she was having on the ranch. She was exuberant in her account of the riding trips, hiking over the rimrock, and also the swimming in Crooked River. This last sport horrified her family. They had visited their friends, the Sharps, briefly in the early days. At that time Central Oregon was often referred to as "typhoid country"—shallow wells in the back yards, livestock tramping around, no sanitation of any kind, and everything undesirable dumped into Crooked River. Margaret Sharp still remembered those times.

When one such letter from Becks arrived, Margaret Sharp was having dinner with her good friends, Becks' mother and father. She listened as the letter was read, then exclaimed:

"Swimming in Crooked River! All those children? Great heavens, that's a typhoid river!"

"Well, we'll do something about that right away," was Mr. Wood's comment, and he promptly did . . . In his return letter to his daughter, Mr. Wood issued a stern ultimatum, "Stay out of that river!"

Becks was heartbroken and wrote, "Won't you change your mind, Dad? It isn't much fun sitting on the bank watching all the others swimming."

From then on, letters continued to fly back and forth between father and daughter. Finally, and after much deliberation, Mr. Wood came to the following conclusion:

161

"Since the swimming parties mean so much to you, Becks, and are such an important part of the daily program and everyone seems to have survived the swimming in the river, I am reconsidering the matter. You will be allowed to swim, but only under one condition—that is that you always keep your head out of the water!"

This last letter relieved a rather unhappy situation, but the postscript caused some amusement. "If the woman in charge up there has five children, she must have some sense." For the first time in my life, I learned it took sense to have five children!

With the depression past and times beginning to improve, we would be able to take life a little easier. Crops were good, the dairy was flourishing, and a new prosperity was in the offing. . . . And we were prepared to meet the challenges to come; the Junior Dude Ranch had revived the pioneer spirit which had brought us west in the first place.

The Junior Dude Ranch had proved a success. We continued to operate it as a thriving business for three seasons. In fact, it became such a popular Central Oregon attraction that we found we couldn't accommodate all the requests for reservations. Finally, the work involved became overwhelming, and the Dude Ranch closed at the end of the third successful season. The venture had served its purpose well, but the ranch crew needed a respite. Perhaps at some future date we might again pick it up, depending on conditions.

23. Sunset

The years following the Dude Ranch—from 1933 through to Pearl Harbor—were the Happy Days. Hal's projects were developing well and so were the children. The days between the thirties and the forties saw all five of them going through the upper grades and on through college—Harry, Tom and Bebs at the University of Oregon and Sam and Jean at Reed College. Those were the Gay Days for the younger generation, and Hal and I often joined them, remembering the parties of our early days on the ranch.

The big house resounded to the noise of boys and girls coming and going. Music echoed through the house at all hours. Horses and riders galloped back and forth over the ranch. Sometimes a rider would be brought in from a bad spill; however, accidents or near tragedies affected us only temporarily, and gaiety was suspended for short intervals only. In the 1930s, the big house drew friends like a beacon.

There were many parties, some for the high school students, others for the college group. Christmas and New Year's Eve parties were highlights of the winter season with all the children home. The furniture in the hall and dining room would be moved out onto the big front porch, and in the living room there would be only a couch and chair here and there. All three rooms would be lighted by their fireplaces and a few candles. The dining room was strictly for dancing. Settles* on each side of

*Wooden benches alongside the fireplace, which was equipped with an iron crane and hanging kettle.

the hall fireplace furnished ample space for those sitting out a dance. Local orchestras were hired to play for the parties, just as our own three had once played.

During the holidays I would partially open the curtains between the dining room and hall and, in the middle of the doorway, would hang a bunch of mistletoe. A pretty little girl once came up to me at one of these parties. Very embarrassed, she asked me if I would come out to the kitchen; she wanted to speak to me. "What's on your mind, Sally?" I asked. Hesitatingly, she whispered, "Oh, Mrs. McCall, would you please hang the mistletoe somewhere else in the room in a darker spot?

Every year when high school closed in the late spring, we invited the faculty to gather on the ranch for a "Field Day." We all looked forward to this gathering. Those who were invited asked others in turn, and through the years the "Field Day" grew and became a tradition.

The big ranch house was always on exhibition from attic to main floor. Touring parties wandered back and forth, with the ladies especially interested in the interior. The men would usually bowl on the green after only a short tour of the house.

It was during one of these Field Days that Bebs rushed up to me and said, "Oh, Mother, the ladies have discovered your evening dresses up in the playroom. They have them out and are practically modeling them." Hal, who was standing near me, said rather stiffly, "Well, I don't know that I care about this, Dote. Do you really think they should be dragging out your clothes?"

"Oh, don't mind, Dad," Bebs broke in, "Mother's so old, it really doesn't matter." I assumed she meant the clothes!

During one of these spring gatherings, I stopped on my way upstairs as I noticed a cluster of women in the dining room. The Tiffany tea service, which Father had replaced after that first disastrous fire, was on the mahogany table by the east window. Our good friend, Chad Irvin from Chicago and Redmond, was delivering a little talk on the silver. I couldn't help hearing part of his speech: "Look closely at this silver, ladies, for you will probably never see anything like it again. All the beautiful work on these pieces is done by hand."

Entertaining crowds of people, young and old, summer and winter, became such a definite part of our lives that I learned to plan ahead for the unexpected guests as well as the expected. In warm weather, we served a cold drink concocted of gallons of tea, sugar, and lemonade—which could be made at almost a moment's notice. My favorite spice cookies were mixed ahead of time and stored in the refrigerator. I could quickly take out the dough, shape the cookies, bake them, and serve them in no time. If the weather was cold, hot cocoa topped with whipped cream took only a short time to prepare; then the big silver tray would be loaded and carried in to the guests.

It was when Sam and Jean were at Reed College that the house was painted. The twins were popular and boys and girls from Reed visited off and on through the summer. A good friend of Hal's and mine from Portland, who was in the paint business, had given us paint for the house during one visit; the house had begun to look rather shabby. With free paint we readily solved the labor situation. The twins' friends were cordially invited to visit at any time that summer—but upon one condition—that they work half the day painting the house; the rest of the time they were free.

In those happy years none of us could foresee the tragedies of the 1940s and a second World War. . . . But as we gradually emerged from the war, Hal felt the load lightening and began looking forward to enjoying the coming years. By that time the machine age had come to the ranch: no more work horses, wagons, and great bread-loaf haystacks. In place of the eight-man and twelve-horse teams, we now had two tractors and baled hay.

It was shortly after the close of the war, in November 1946, that Hal turned to his youngest son, Sam, and said, "You know, Sammy, for the first time since the 1920s we're out of the red."

Here the story should end—but life is not like that. On February 1, 1947, Hal McCall died of a coronary thrombosis.

He died quickly in his own bed, at home on the ranch he had created. In his determination to make a success of the ranch, Hal had weathered many storms and overcome many hardships. His eastern background and his abiding sense of fair play had carried him through heartbreaking experiences. Yet, down through the years, he never lost a certain spirit of gaiety:

> Always leave them laughing when you say good-by,
>> Never linger long about,
>> Never wear your welcome out,
> Always leave them laughing when you say good-by.

That old song was a favorite of Hal's.

The End

Photographs

The Author as a young girl ready for a ride.

Thomas W. Lawson—the Wall Street financier who fell in love with Central Oregon.

Hal's father, Samuel W. McCall, Governor of Massachusetts and United States Congressman.

Dreamwold in winter—the main residence on the estate of the Author's father, Thomas W. Lawson, at Cape Cod, Massachusetts.

The Author's father, mother, and sister Bunny (Jean), in coach at Dreamwold.

The Wickersham Apartments at Northwest 18th and Flanders, in Portland. This was the McCalls' first "home" in the West.

Hal and Dorothy McCall on their Central Oregon ranch in 1911. Hal's handkerchief on the sagebrush marks the site of their future home.

Tom Lawson and Tom Sharp on the nearby Sharp ranch.

The Prineville Baseball Team around 1913. Front row: Sam Ellis, unidentified player, J. Young, Fod Mason, and Lake Bechtell. Back row: Jess Tetherow, Hal McCall, two unidentified players, Ed McFarland, and Slim Yancey. (Names furnished by Lake Bechtell).

The Central Oregon ranch house under construction in 1912. Photo was taken from the top of the rimrock.

Three wagons loaded with the family belongings which escaped the fire at Redmond in 1912.

Hauling pipe for the irrigation system in 1912. The driver rides the wheel horse with only one line to the lead horse. He jerks the line and calls the orders; this is known as a "jerk line."

Wagons used in the ranch harvest during the autumn of 1912.

Big Billy—total livestock on the ranch in 1912.

The nearest "store" in 1911 was a combination saloon, post office and trading center at O'Neil, Oregon.

Dorothy's sister Bunny watches the harvest of the first grain crop; the threshing machine and "crew."

Team of six horses hauling harvested grain below the rimrock.

The first alfalfa crop (1913) on the ranch under the rimrock.

Hal, Harry, and a passing Canadian trapper about 1913.

The first winter at the ranch—a snow-covered world.

"Dote" McCall in mid-air. "On this aerial bridge we crossed Crooked River to meet the stage from Prineville to pick up provisions. Later a bridge was built."

Second Christmas on the ranch: Harry is riding "Peg" and Baby Tom watches from chair. Pegasus was a Christmas present from Grandfather Lawson.

Minnie I. Haggart—nurse, friend, and loyal companion—was "Miss Ha" to all the McCalls.

The tin pig houses are on the right. From these too-small quarters came the daily, disastrous pig reports to the Wall Street financier.

Florence Idella Sharp in 1916—world champion butterfat producer—with Bebs on board.

Grandfather Lawson, Harry, and friends at Alma Howe's Cottage Farm Resort in Hood River, Oregon. This was a frequently used stop-over between the McCall ranch and Portland.

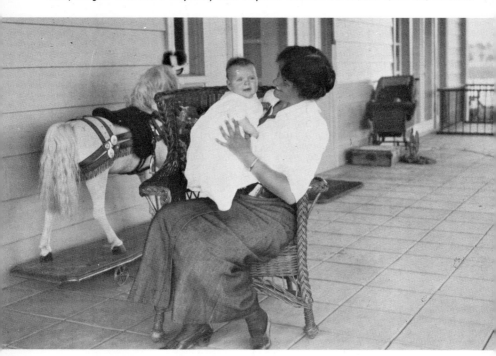

Dorothy Lawson McCall and daughter, Bebs. "Peg" idles in the background.

Dorothy and Bebs flanked by Harry and Tom—on the front lawn.

The Prohibition Twins—Sam and Jean.

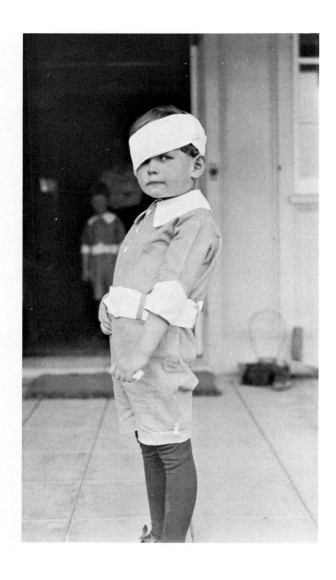

Tommy McCall as a World War I wounded hero—after colliding with a closed glass door.

Three cheers for the red, white, and blue! Tom and Harry in 1918, with Bebs, "the littlest soldier."

Dorothy's brother, Douglas, visits Westernwold—
and gets a ranch of his own.

Hal and Dorothy, 30 years after the handkerchief was placed on the sagebrush.

Prineville vs. Bend Tennis Tournament in 1912. From left: Mrs. George P. Putnam, George P.
Putnam, J. P. Keyes, and C. S. Hudson, of Bend; A R. Bowman, Lake Bechtell, Fay Baldwin,
Dorothy McCall, Hal McCall, Ray Brewster, and Dr. J. H. Rosenberg, of Prineville. (Names
furnished by Lake Bechtell)

Bebs McCall riding herd on Holstein dairy cattle beside Crooked River at low water.

The little white Montgomery schoolhouse, District 18, where the McCall children went to grade school, riding bareback on their own horses.

Harry, Tom, and Bebs McCall, ready for a hockey game. When the sloughs froze over—and sometimes the river—the family organized its own hockey teams.

The children made their own fun on the ranch under the rimrock. Here, Harry on the horse is pulling Tom on skis.

By 1921, Hal McCall had established a dairy herd which became the foundation of Central Oregon's dairy industry.

The young McCalls in 1933--Sam, Bebs, Tom, Harry and Jean.

Tom McCall—Oregon's future governor—pitches hay at Westernwold. "All the children worked on the ranch."

This buck-rake and haying crew shows how hay was harvested on the ranch in the twenties and early thirties.

The hall fireplace at Westernwold. Hal's golf and tennis trophies are on the mantel. The guns reflect the extensive hunting (for predators and game birds) that was part of every-day life on the ranch . . . the room looks much the same today, when three generations of McCalls come to visit.

Looking across the hall from the living room to the dining room. Under the bronze lion, note the pictures of the 1909 baseball team at Harvard—Hal's alma mater.

The McCall Ranch today—shown from the air looking east. Crooked River winds to the right.

A closer aerial view. Note the ranch buildings in the background and the rimrock towering over all. Situated in the Crooked River Valley, halfway between Redmond and Prineville, the McCall Ranch lies between the Cascades and the Blue Mountains.